MESSENGERS OF GOD

A Survey of Old Testament Prophets

KIERAN LARKIN

Copyright © 2020 by Kieran Larkin

Published by Red Penguin Books

ISBN

Print 978-1-949864-26-7

Digital 978-1-949864-27-4

All rights reserved.

No part of this book may be reproduced in any form or by any electronic or mechanical means, including information storage and retrieval systems, without written permission from the author, except for the use of brief quotations in a book review.

TABLE OF CONTENTS

Chapter 1:   Introduction to the Prophets   1

                    Prophets of the Monarchy

Chapter 2:   Samuel   13

Chapter 3:   Nathan   25

                    Prophets of the Divided Kingdom

Chapter 4:   Elijah   33

Chapter 5:   Elisha   45

Chapter 6:   Amos   59

Chapter 7:   Hosea   69

Chapter 8:   Isaiah   81

Chapter 9:   Micah   107

Prophets of the Exile

Chapter 10:	Ezekiel	115
Chapter 11:	Jeremiah	131
Chapter 12:	Daniel	151
Chapter 13:	Jonah	177

Additional Prophets of Note

Chapter 14:	The Remaining "Minor" Prophets	187
Chapter 15:	Joel	189
Chapter 16:	Obadiah	193
Chapter 17:	Nahum	197
Chapter 18:	Habakkuk	201
Chapter 19:	Zephaniah	205
Chapter 20:	Haggai	209
Chapter 21:	Zechariah	213
Chapter 22:	Malachi	219

About the Author

PREFACE

It's been my privilege to serve as a teacher of religious studies for the past forty years, first in a Catholic parochial school, and second in a prestigious Catholic high school. Teaching religion has been an incredibly fulfilling experience for me, and while I have occasionally taught other subjects as well, nothing has offered me the same degree of satisfaction.

Over the course of time I have taught a number of different courses in the general field of religious studies - courses on Catholic doctrine, morality, social justice, Christology, spirituality, bereavement and comparative religions - but it was in teaching a course on the Bible that the roots of this book were planted.

There are many, many theologians who are rightly labeled Biblical experts or scholars. I am not among them. Rather, I'm a simple layperson who finds the Bible both fascinating and inspirational, and would like to share those sentiments with others. And I guess that when I use such words as "fascinating" and "inspirational," those words are perfect to express my feelings about the prophets whose words and deeds dot the landscape of the *Hebrew Scriptures*, what we Christians now call the *Old Testament*.

When I was much younger, my own religious studies teachers would mention the prophets, but they never seemed to place a great deal of emphasis on them. Other aspects of our faith were a higher priority. So over the course of time I recognized the names of many of the Old Testament prophets, but that's as far as it went. I knew little to nothing about their personal lives, the messages they delivered or the audiences they addressed. They were two-dimensional cardboard cutouts devoid of depth and definition. But as I grew older (and hopefully a little more mature), my interest in them began to pique - and I wanted to know them a little better.

I think it's not an uncommon reality that many people tend to lump all of the prophets together as if they are largely interchangeable - delivering the same message(s) in the same way(s) to the same people(s). Yet I've discovered that nothing could be further from the truth!

It is my hope that those who may read this book will come to see that the prophets of the Old Testament are as unique and individual as we are today. While it's true that the messages they conveyed to their audiences as commissioned by God all reflected several similar themes, that's where the similarity begins and ends. When each prophet is "fleshed out," it becomes quite clear that each had his (or her) own individual style, own personal problems, own limitations, and own audience to address.

Another observation that rings true is that one's service to God as a prophet was no proverbial "walk in the park." While we may rightly consider it an honor to be called by God to serve as His messenger, it was not uncommon for the life of a prophet to be filled with all sorts of angst and pain - including loneliness, persecution, rejection, physical torture, imprisonment, despair, self-doubt, and even death. Delivering messages to a population that doesn't want to hear them is no easy task. Individuals who responded positively to God's call and willingly subjected themselves to the abandonment or abuse they were likely to receive were nothing less than heroic, and their lives should be viewed through the prism of their faith and dedication.

I guess that's why I chose to write this book - to present the prophets of the Old Testament as the genuine heroes they were: as normal folk - just like us - who received an extraordinary call to God's service and responded (sometimes with great trepidation, I admit) with courage and commitment and absolute fidelity. Their exploits may be over two thousand years old, but they can still serve as role models and inspirational paradigms for us today.

This book doesn't even try to present *all* of the Old Testament prophets who are mentioned by name in Scripture. Such research and composition is beyond my limitations. So in this book I've selected a cross-section of my "favorites" who span the era of Jewish history from the Age of Judges to the Babylonian Exile. I think they constitute a very interesting and dynamic cadre, and they make a good starting point for anyone who wishes to study the prophets more comprehensively. This doesn't mean that the prophets I've omitted are less important or interesting - not at all. Perhaps if I find another book within me, they'll be presented with the prominence they so richly deserve. My hope is that this book serves as a catalyst for more depthful exploration, as it really only scratches the surface of the rich legacy left by the prophets of the Old Testament.

The translation I have used throughout this book comes from the *Good News Bible: Today's English Version*, published by the American Bible Society in 1976 (Imprimatur: Archbishop John Francis Whealon of Hartford). I find its use of vocabulary and grammar to be eminently readable and contemporary. I have been faithful to it in all ways but one: I made it a point to capitalize all references to God (i.e. His, Lord, Spirit, etc.) out of profound respect for the Almighty. In this day and age when we strive to be all-inclusive and "politically correct," it's not lost on me that God transcends all gender designations and limitations, thereby making masculine references less than accurate. But I've decided that, in this book, I'm prioritizing respect over gender accuracy. Author's prerogative!

One final two-part note: I always thought that writing a book was somewhat beyond my capabilities. Perhaps this book is my "one and only." We'll see. But I want to single out the members of my family -

and especially my wife Stephanie - for their words of encouragement and support of my efforts during the months this text was researched and composed. Stephanie has it in her head that I can do practically anything (she's mistaken, of course!), but I'd like her to hold onto that misconception a little bit longer. If you're reading these words, then I accomplished a feat I never thought was in me, and I'm humbled and grateful for that. But I also want to acknowledge my colleagues in the field of religious studies as well. I've spent the last 36 years as a religious studies teacher at The Mary Louis Academy in Jamaica Estates, New York - a prestigious all-girls Catholic high school administered by the Sisters of St. Joseph of Brentwood, New York. All of my colleagues dazzle me daily with their expertise, their dedication and their professionalism, but the members of my own religious studies department - with whom I work most closely - radiate a profound level of faith and devotion to God, as well as an equally profound sense of responsibility to introduce the love of God to our students - that they truly inspire me each and every day. So I also wish to acknowledge my dynamic colleagues Laura, Mike, Caitlin, Josephine, Erin and Loramarie - and their immediate predecessors Kellie, Katie, Pat, Jean, Marie and Joan. Enveloped by my family's love and energized by my fellow teachers' faith, I dedicate this book to all of them.

Chapter One
INTRODUCTION TO THE PROPHETS

If ever a word conjured up multiple images and generated a cornucopia of synonyms, it would be the word *prophet*. Never has a single noun been applied to a wider cast of characters ranging through the ancient mists of yesteryear to today's media prognosticators. But to even begin to address the whole of this litany of individuals would be to cast a net far too wide for one book to address properly. So in the interest of succinctness and conservatism, I'd like to confine this text to the most common usage of the word - as it applies to a number of quite dynamic and diverse personalities whose words and exploits dominate so much of what we call today the *Hebrew Scriptures* or the Christian *Old Testament*.

In Hebrew, the word *nabi* describes the role of what we today call a "prophet." *Nabi* literally means to "bubble up" - describing one within whom the touch of God is generating a kind of spiritual effervescence. A nabi, then, was one who spoke for God, who delivered the messages of God with accuracy, urgency and passion to God's Chosen People, the Israelites. Our English word *prophet* is derived from the Greek *prophetes*, meaning "one who declares the divine will."

The Hebrew Scriptures have a great deal to say about this prophetic calling - and list over 130 prophets by name (not to mention scores of unnamed prophets - and whole prophetic "schools" - as well). Prophets came from many different backgrounds, were called to their ministry in many different ways, and delivered a variety of different messages to God's People. Most were men, perhaps understandably so in a male-dominated world of three millennia ago, but some were women (Deborah, Huldah, Miriam, Anna). And while some were entrusted by God with the performance of a single task - to convey His message with fervor and accuracy - still others were required to juggle several full-time tasks (or wear several hats, as it were) as they "doubled" as judges, priests, farmers and herders. In the broadest possible sense, any individual who delivered any message from God to anyone else can be defined as a prophet. So Patriarchs such as Abraham and Moses can be, and have been, defined rightly as prophets alongside others who primary role was something other than prophetic.

As theologian William P. Roberts of the University of Dayton pointed out in his 1981 book *The Prophets Speak Today*, "The Hebrew prophets were impassioned persons who intimately experienced God and who were consumed with a deep love and concern for His people. As a consequence, they anguished over the plight of the Israelites in times of crisis...This zeal led the prophets to cry out the message of God to the people of their day."

In today's world, even a casual observer of "Judaica/Christianica" will be familiar with the names of some of the Old Testament prophets: Jeremiah, Isaiah, Ezekiel and Elijah spring to mind almost immediately. Other names such as Elisha, Amos, Hosea and Micah might place a distant second. And I wouldn't bet on Obadiah, Habakkuk, Nahum or Zephaniah to win, place or show! The fact is that the Old Testament offers a great deal of specific information about some of the prophets, but provides scant details about others. And what about other Biblical personages whose notoriety comes from accomplishments far different from the delivery of God's messages? Was the Adam of Genesis a prophet? What about Noah? (Islam, by the way, affirms both as prophets!) What about Methuselah? What about Enoch?

Biblical scholars and exegetes far more accomplished than I have sought to identify a series of common threads that in some way link or unite the prophets in regard to shared characteristics. They've developed such a list, although they would have to admit that the application of this list to all of the prophets is simply impossible - too much personal information is missing from the Scriptures to apply universally. Nevertheless, there is a general agreement that the prophets authentically chosen by God to convey His messages - whether the Scriptural details to verify these threads exist or not - all received "the prophetic call" and employed a "messenger formula."

THE PROPHETIC CALL

Each prophet is individually called by God in a way that is compelling and dramatic. For Moses, God spoke to him through the theophany of the burning bush. Samuel heard the voice of God while sleeping. Ezekiel saw a vision. Jeremiah encountered God in his dreams. In each case, the experience was sufficiently intense and personal enough that there was no doubt as to its divine origin.

Biblical scholars also present this compelling call as merely the first stage in a five-step process that cements the relationship between the prophet and God that leads ultimately to the prophet completing his mission.

If stage one can be labeled *the lure*, which commands the attention of the prophet, then stage two would be *the commission*, wherein God articulates the assignment with which He entrusts His prophet. In the case of Moses, it was the burning bush that first piqued Moses' interest:

> *The angel of the Lord appeared to him as a flame coming from the middle of a bush. Moses saw that the bush was on fire but that it was not burning up. "This is strange," he thought. "Why isn't the bush burning up? I will go closer and see." (Ex 3:2-3)*

But when Moses approached the bush to investigate the phenomenon further, this "lure" was soon followed by "the commission," God's enlistment of Moses to address Pharaoh and establish himself as the spokesperson and leader of the enslaved Hebrews.

> *Now I am sending you to the king of Egypt so that you can lead My people out of his country. (Ex 3:10)*

The third stage, called *the resistance*, is the prophet's refusal to accept the assignment, usually by offering one or more excuses, citing either unfitness or unworthiness. Moses desperately threw up roadblocks as impediments to this calling:

> *I am nobody… (Ex 3:11)*

> *Suppose the Israelites do not believe me and will not listen…" (Ex 4:1)*

> *I have never been a good speaker…I am a poor speaker, slow and hesitant. (Ex 4:10)*

These attempts to "pass the buck" are turned aside in stage four (*the reassurance*), when God allays the doubts of those He called. God's responses to Moses quelled his fears, at least up to a point:

> *I will be with you… (Ex 3:12)*

> *My people will listen to what you have to say to them. (Ex 3:18)*

> *I will help you to speak, and I will tell you what to say. (Ex 4:12)*

If these reassurances weren't enough, God also empowered Moses to provide three demonstrations of his authority - turning a walking stick into a snake (Ex 4:2-5), afflicting his own hand with disease and curing it instantaneously (Ex 4:6-7), and turning Nile water into blood (Ex 4:9). He even allowed Moses' brother Aaron to accompany him to Pharaoh's court for both moral and verbal support.

With all roadblocks removed, the path was clear for Moses to commence stage 5 (*the resolution*) and fulfill his divine assignment.

This five-stage call cannot be applied to each of the Old Testament prophets from what is presently known to us through Scripture, but other examples will present themselves in the lives of several subsequent prophets whose lives and messages we will explore.

THE MESSENGER FORMULA

In Old Testament times, the vast majority of the people were illiterate - and this included many of the people who were chosen to deliver messages, whether those messages were from the local monarch or lord (as delivered by heralds) or by God (as delivered by prophets). For this reason, the messengers needed to memorize the text of their messages and deliver them orally. Therefore, it was necessary to employ a phrase of introduction to differentiate to the recipients of the message when the messenger was speaking for himself and when he was repeating the words of the author of the message.

In the case of many of the prophets, this "messenger formula" took several similar forms. Ezekiel would introduce his message with the formula, ""The Sovereign Lord said…" (Ez 25:8,12,15) or "The Lord spoke to me…" (Ez 24:1,15) The same was true of Amos, "The Sovereign Lord says…" (Am 3:4) or "The Lord says..." (Am 3:10,12) and Hosea, "The Lord says…" (Ho 7:3,8) Zechariah would begin with the words, "The Lord Almighty says…" (Zec 8:20) or "This is the Lord's message…" (Zec 9:1) All of these formulae were quite similar, and the reality is that false prophets could employ them as well. As a matter of fact, the Old Testament is littered with the names of false prophets who tried to pass themselves off as the "real McCoy." An obvious example is Hananiah, the son of Azzur, who falsely claimed to speak for God in the court of King Zedekiah of Judah during the time of Jeremiah (Jr 28:1-17). There were, of course, many, many others as well. Nevertheless, these formulae were an accepted, and perhaps necessary, convention used to indicate the specific message of its author. It was up to the people, of course, to accept or reject the authenticity of each prophet.

It has also become something of a convention to categorize the Old Testament prophets in a variety of ways, usually based on such issues as the length of their writings, the placement of their ministries in the corpus of the Hebrew Scriptures, or the historical setting that served as the backdrop for their messages.

MAJOR AND MINOR PROPHETS

This designation is probably the most misunderstood classification of prophets because of its misapplication (by today's standards) of the terms "major" and "minor." We generally employ these two words to convey the relative importance of a topic or issue - that which is "major" holds special significance; that which is "minor" is merely ancillary or tangential. In Old Testament parlance, however, these designations do not describe the importance of the prophet's message, the issues it addresses nor the urgency of its delivery. Rather, it relates to the length of the prophet's writings and pronouncements. Therefore, Isaiah, Jeremiah and Ezekiel are considered *Major Prophets* because the books ascribe to them are of considerable length. The Book of Lamentations is also listed here as it is thought to have been composed by Jeremiah.

The *Minor Prophets* - Hosea, Joel, Amos, Jonah, Obadiah, Micah, Nahum, Habakkuk, Zephaniah, Haggai, Zechariah and Malachi - have earned their classification simply on the shorter length of their works. Their collective writings were originally placed in the Hebrew Scriptures in one book - the "Book of the Twelve" - so they are sometimes grouped together under that name - "The Twelve."

It should also be noted that there are other classifications of some of the prophets. For example, Samuel, Nathan, Abijah, Elijah and Elisha are referred to as the *Oral Prophets* or *Speaking Prophets* because their prophecies were not written down nor are books of Scripture named after them. This list is often expanded to include Abraham and the other Patriarchs of Israel, some of the Judges, and other personages whose words and actions are detailed in some of the Historical Books of Scripture, such as 1st and 2nd Samuel, 1st and 2nd Chronicles and 1st and 2nd Kings. Prophets whose writings are presented in Scriptural Books named after them are called *Writing Prophets* by contrast.

Another categorization of the prophets delineates between the *Former Prophets* and the *Latter Prophets*. The Former Prophets are those prophets whose words and deeds occurred before the time of the Divided Kingdom (circa 930 BCE), while the Latter Prophets ministered after the schism that created the separate nations of Israel and Judah.

This book is organized along chronological, historical lines and groups prophets according to the time period in which they delivered their messages. Therefore, some prophets are identified as *Prophets of the Monarchy* if their ministries unfolded during the time of Kings Saul, David and Solomon, while others are labeled *Prophets of the Divided Kingdom* if they prophesied when the Chosen People split into the two separate kingdoms of Israel and Judah. The *Prophets of the Exile* ministered during and after the Babylonian Exile of the sixth century BCE, and the *Additional Prophets of Note* include the remaining Minor Prophets who were not discussed previously in separate chapters.

CHAPTER 1: QUESTIONS FOR REVIEW

1. What is meant by the Hebrew word *nabi*?
2. How many prophets can be found in the Old Testament?
3. What are the five elements found in the *prophetic call*? Explain each in their proper order.
4. How were these elements displayed in God's call to Moses?
5. Why did prophets display a *messenger formula*? Give three examples of this formula.
6. What is the difference between a *major prophet* and a *minor prophet*? Which prophets are found ineach designation?
7. What differentiates *speaking prophets* from *writing prophets*?
8. When did the *former prophets* deliver God's messages? When did the *latter prophets* deliver them?

PROPHETS OF THE MONARCHY

Chapter Two
SAMUEL

"Speak, Lord, Your servant is listening"

The prophet Samuel was an individual who wore three hats - as prophet, priest and judge (in that order). It was Samuel who served as a bridge from the Age of Judges to the establishment of the Israelite monarchy under Kings Saul and David.

Samuel was born in 1064 BCE in the village of Ramah in the hill country of Ephraim. His father Elkanah was a devout Levite (according to the genealogical listing in 1 Chronicles 6:22) who had two wives - not at all uncommon for that time period and culture. Elkanah's first wife was Hannah, but Hannah bore him no children, so after ten years, Elkanah took a second wife, Peninnah, who did bear him several offspring. Hannah was Elkanah's favorite wife - which Peninnah knew - so a rivalry was created due to Peninnah's jealousy of Hannah. As a result, Peninnah incessantly ridiculed and berated Hannah because of her barrenness.

At this time, the ancient Samaritan city of Shiloh was a major spiritual center for the Israelites, serving as home to the Ark of the Covenant, an honor it held for over 300 years before the Ark was captured by the Philistines. Therefore, it was Elkanah's custom, as a spiritually observant Levite, to bring his family to Shiloh for regular religious pilgrimages at the temple. At this time, the shrine at Shiloh was administered by the High Priest Eli, assisted by his two nefarious sons Hophni and Phinehas. Eli also served the Israelites as one of their judges, following the tenure of his predecessor, Samson.

During one of these pilgrimages to Shiloh, Peninnah's continual harassment of Hannah reduced her to a state of tearful despair. She entered the temple precincts where, through bitter tears, she prayed silently while moving her lips. Eli observed her from the entrance to the temple and, believing her to be drunk, began to reprimand her. When Hannah unburdened herself to Eli - telling him of her troubles with Peninnah, her desire to have a child, and her willingness to offer this child to the service of God in gratitude, Eli recognized his error in judgment, blessed her, and added his prayer to hers.

Go in peace, and may the God of Israel give you what you have asked him for. (1 Samuel 1:17)

Hannah returned to Elkanah with her spirit somewhat lifted, returned home, and soon found herself pregnant. She gave birth to a son and named him Samuel, which means "son of God" and is related to the Hebrew word for "ask" - because she asked God to grant her a child.

Once Hannah had weaned Samuel, she returned to Shiloh and presented him to Eli to fulfill the promise she had made to offer her son to God's service. From this time onward, Samuel remained at Shiloh in the house of Eli to complete his training for the priesthood.

A word must be said at this point about Hophni and Phinehas, the sons of Eli. As priests, they left much to be desired. One of the primary duties of the priests at Shiloh was to officiate at the sacrifices pilgrims wished to make to God. Hophni and Phinehas violated the rules guaranteeing the sanctity of the sacrifices, stole from the people whose sacrifices they were supervising, and slept with the young women who helped to care for the temple precincts. As Eli grew older, he found it more difficult to control his sons. He attempted to reprimand them, but they ignored him and continued to violate their sacred duties. The Lord grew very displeased with their lack of respect as well as with Eli's inability to curtail their evil ways.

While all of this drama was unfolding, Samuel continued to grow and to learn the ways of the priesthood - and found favor with God as well as with the people. However, it was the improprieties of Hophni and Phinehas that led directly to Samuel's call to be a prophet.

Shortly before Samuel's dramatic call narrative began, a prophet (for whom no name is mentioned in Scripture) approached Eli with a message from the Lord. He told Eli that God was greatly displeased with the evil and disrespectful behavior of Hophni and Phinehas as well as with Eli's inability to control them. Therefore it was the Lord's intention to punish the house of Eli. Although they were direct descendants of Aaron and were perpetually entrusted with the responsibility of serving as the Lord's priests, He would rescind this honor and deprive the young men of Eli's family with long life. Other Israelite families would receive the blessings of the Lord and serve Him as priests, and Eli would see both of his sons die on the same day as a demonstration of the veracity of this prophecy.

SAMUEL'S CALL NARRATIVE

Shortly thereafter, when Samuel was about eleven years of age and still receiving his priestly training in the house of Eli, he had a transformative spiritual experience (his "call narrative") late one night. While Eli, now severely visually impaired due to his old age, slept in his bedchamber, Samuel was also asleep in the temple sanctuary near the Ark of the Covenant. The Lord called to Samuel, who replied "Yes, sir" and ran to Eli's bedchamber, thinking it was Eli who had summoned him. Eli responded "My son, I didn't call you. Go back to bed." This scenario repeated itself two more times, and Eli realized that it was the Lord who was calling out to Samuel. He advised Samuel, if he heard the voice again, to respond by saying

> *Speak, Lord. Your servant is listening. (1 Samuel 3:9)*

According to the First Book of Samuel (3:10), the Lord then appeared to Samuel and called him by name again. When Samuel answered Him as instructed by Eli, the Lord repeated to Samuel the dire predictions (threats) that the previous unnamed prophet had already made to Eli about the Lord's displeasure with Eli and his sons and His plans to punish Eli's family. In the morning, Samuel was afraid to repeat to Eli the details of his vision of the Lord, but Eli insisted that he hold nothing back.

> *Don't keep anything from me. God will punish you severely if you don't tell me everything He said. (1 Samuel 3:17)*

So Samuel repeated the Lord's message - sparing no details - and Eli realized that God had chosen Samuel to be a prophet. It was impossible for Samuel to know such details unless they had been revealed to him by the Lord, for Eli had told no one else of the predictions already conveyed to him by the previous prophet.

Samuel continued to learn and to mature, and the Lord continued to speak with him and guide him. Samuel grew in stature as a prophet to whom the Israelites would listen. It happened one day that the deaths of Hophni and Phinehas, as foretold to Samuel, came to pass at the Battle of Aphek in 1024 BCE. In this skirmish, the Israelites were defeated by the Philistines, who also captured the Ark of the Covenant. Upon hearing of the death of his two sons and the loss of the Ark, the elderly Eli fell backwards in his grief, broke his neck, and died as well.

The presence of the Ark of the Covenant in the Philistine city of Ashdod (later transported to the other Philistine cities of Gath and Ekron) caused great distress and suffering to the Philistines, as the Lord punished them with "tumors" (possibly caused by bubonic plague) for their theft of the Ark. The Philistines eventually returned the Ark to the Israelites, where it resided in the city of Kiriath-Jearim for twenty years. Samuel convinced the Israelites of the necessity of returning to exclusive worship of Yahweh, as dictated by the Covenant, so the Israelites destroyed the idols they had created to false gods like the Canaanite god and goddess Baal and Astarte. Samuel continued to lead the Israelites throughout his entire lifetime. Through his prayers, sacrifices and closeness to God, Samuel enabled the Israelites not only to repel Philistine attacks, but also to rout them in battle and regain territories previously lost to them (1 Samuel 7-13). He traveled throughout the land of the Israelites, settling disputes as judge and leader.

Unfortunately, Samuel experienced a painful episode in his own life that paralleled that of his mentor Eli. As Samuel grew older, he appointed his sons Joel and Abijah to serve as judges, thereby relieving him of some of his responsibilities. But, like the sons of Eli, their greed led them astray from the moral path they were supposed to follow into the acceptance of bribes and rendering of dishonorable and unfair judicial decisions.

The other local leaders throughout Israel were fearful of the future ministrations of these two and sought change. They complained to Samuel:

> *Look, you are getting old and your sons don't follow your example. So, then, appoint a king to rule over us...as other countries have. (1 Samuel 8:5)*

It should be noted here that at this point in their history, the Israelites viewed God as their king, and looked upon the Lord as the One Who would vanquish their enemies and watch over them in perpetuity. Consequently, they referred to their human leaders as "judges" rather than as "kings" - their judges serving more as tribal military leaders than as courtroom mediators, as we use the term today. It was through the efforts of such judges as Joshua, Othniel, Ehud, Shamgar, Deborah, Gideon, Tola, Jair, Jephthah, Ibzan, Elon, Abdon and Samson (all of whom are listed in the Book of Judges as predecessors of Eli and Samuel) that the Israelites were able to secure a homeland for themselves within the land of Canaan after Moses gained their release from slavery in Egypt.

Samuel was greatly distressed by this request for a king, viewing it as a personal insult, and brought his upsetment to the Lord. The Lord advised Samuel not to view this as a rejection of him as judge.

> *You are not the one they have rejected; I am the one they have rejected as their king. Ever since I brought them out of Egypt, they have turned away from Me and worshipped other gods; and now they are doing to you what they have always done to Me. (1 Samuel 8:7-8)*

The Lord told Samuel to listen to the people, but also to warn them of how they would be treated by kingly rulers. Samuel complied, with this warning to the Israelites:

> *This is how your king will treat you. He will make soldiers of your sons; some of them will serve in his war chariots, others in his cavalry...Your sons will have to plow his fields, harvest his crops and make his weapons...Your daughters will have to...work as his cooks and his bakers. He will take your*

> *best fields, vineyards and olive groves, and give them to his officials. He will take your servants and your best cattle and donkeys and make them work for him. He will take a tenth of your flocks, and you yourselves will become his slaves... (1 Samuel 8:11-17)*

Despite this dire warning, the Israelites insisted on monarchical rule, and the Lord instructed Samuel to give them what they wanted.

Kish was an affluent and respected man from the tribe of Benjamin, and his son Saul was tall, striking and handsome. It was Saul who was the Lord's choice to be anointed as king. He said to Samuel:

> *Tomorrow I will send you a man from the tribe of Benjamin; anoint him as ruler of my people Israel... (1 Samuel 9:16)*

Samuel did as the Lord instructed. He anointed Saul with olive oil and introduced him to the tribes of Israel as their new king. Many were supportive of him as their new ruler, but others disapproved.

Within a month, King Nahash, the ruler of the Ammonites to the east of Israel, attacked the town of Jabesh on the east shore of the Jordan River in Gilead. When word of this reached King Saul, he marshalled 330,000 soldiers and defeated the Ammonites handily. This decisive response quelled any opposition and cemented his status as king. As the Israelites celebrated their victory, Samuel took the opportunity to remind the Israelites of their responsibilities to God. He said:

> *Here is the king you chose; you asked for him and now the Lord has given him to you. All will go well with you if you honor the Lord your God, serve Him, listen to Him, and obey His commands...if you and your king follow him. But if you...disobey His commands, He will be against you and your king....Do not turn away from the Lord, but serve Him with all your heart. Don't go after false gods; they cannot help you or save you, for they are not real....Obey the Lord and serve Him faithfully with all your heart. Remember the great things He has done for you. But if you continue to sin, you and your king will be destroyed. (1 Samuel 12:13-15,20-21,24-25)*

Saul engaged in a series of battles against the other Canaanite tribes surrounding Israel - the Philistines (to the west), Moabites and Edomites (to the southeast), Ammonites (to the east) and Amalekites (to the southwest). Saul's forces were victorious against all of them. But his conflict with the Amalekites - and his failure to follow the directives of God through Samuel - proved to be his undoing, and led to the end of his reign.

The Amalekites had long been an enemy of Israel, and skirmishes between the two tribes had been ongoing for many generations, most probably dating back to Joshua, several hundred years earlier. Samuel approached Saul with specific instructions from the Lord:

> *Go and attack the Amalekites and completely destroy everything they have. Don't leave a thing; kill all the men, women and children and babies; the cattle, sheep, camels and donkeys. (1 Samuel 15:3)*

While this divine assignment seems uncharacteristically brutal and uncompromising, it is reflective of a demand make by God generations earlier - at the time of Moses and Joshua - to erase the Amalekites from existence for their uncompromising opposition to the Israelites upon their emergence from the Red Sea (or "Sea of Reeds"). This call for their complete annihilation is known as *herem* ("the ban"):

> *Remember what the Amalekites did to you as you were coming from Egypt. They had no fear of God, and so they attacked you from the rear when you were tired and exhausted, and killed all who were straggling behind. So then, when the Lord your God has given you the land and made you safe from all your enemies who live around you, be sure to kill all the Amalekites, so that no one will remember them any longer. Do not forget! (Deuteronomy 25:17-19)*

When Saul's forces defeated the Amalekites, he spared the life of Agag, the Amalekite king, and did not kill the best cattle, sheep, calves and lambs, claiming that it was his intention to offer them as a sacrifice to God. But his disobedience to God's command displeased God so much that the Lord regretted His decision to have Samuel anoint Saul as king. When Samuel approached Saul, who was quite pleased with his victory, he informed Saul of God's displeasure: Samuel asked:

> Which does the Lord prefer: obedience or offerings and sacrifices?...Because you rejected the Lord's command, He has rejected you as king. (1 Samuel 15:22-23)

Saul realized his failure at this point and hoped to placate the Lord by worshipping Him and killing Agag, but his fate was already sealed. Samuel left him, returned to his home in Ramah, and never saw Saul again, but Samuel, nevertheless, had one final task to perform. The Lord informed Samuel that He had chosen a new king for Samuel to anoint. Samuel panicked at the thought:

> How can I do that? If Saul hears about it, he will kill me! he pleaded. (1 Samuel 16:2)

But the Lord instructed Samuel to bring the oil for anointing to the village of Bethlehem, where God had chosen one of the sons of Jesse to serve as the next king. It was here that Samuel anointed David, the youngest of eight sons, in the presence of his family. Then Samuel returned to his home in Ramah. Saul was unaware of the anointing of David as his successor.

The upcoming years brought Saul and David into direct contact. David was introduced to Saul as a harpist whose music might soothe the troubled monarch who knew he was no longer in God's favor. But while Saul took kindly to the young David initially, he grew jealous of David when David's victory over the Philistines and their champion Goliath began to overshadow the accomplishments of Saul. The king's envy of David ultimately led to multiple plots on Saul's part to have David executed, all of which failed, but none of which caused David to renounce his loyalty to Saul. At one point, David fled Saul's court and asked Samuel for sanctuary in Ramah. The complicated and tempestuous relationship between Saul and his successor David is the stuff of melodrama, but not central to the story of Samuel as priest, prophet and judge of Israel.

Samuel's place in the history of the Chosen People is of pre-eminent importance. He is the prophet who played a pivotal role in the transition from the *Age of Judges*, during which the Israelites were governed primarily by military chieftains as they sought to establish a homeland for themselves in Canaan, and the establishment of the Israelite monarchy that followed. Samuel's call to prophethood - while still a boy - led him to live a life of total dedication to the Lord and unquestionable moral uprightness and integrity. He never wavered in his resolve to serve the Lord, and God's faithfulness in his servant Samuel was demonstrated by the countless times God spoke directly to Samuel, rather than through intercessors or theophanies. It is said about Samuel that his place in Judaic history stands alongside Moses in stature. No small accomplishment!

.

CHAPTER 2: QUESTIONS FOR REVIEW

1. Who were Samuel's parents? What was the cause of tension in Samuel's family?
2. What role does Eli play in the life of Samuel?
3. What promise did Hannah make to God?
4. Why are Hophni and Phinehas described as "nefarious?" Give examples to justify this description.
5. Describe Samuel's *call narrative*.
6. What problem did Samuel face that paralleled the problem of Eli? How was it resolved?
7. List the names of the Judges of Israel.
8. Why was Samuel upset by the Israelites' request for him to appoint a king?
9. What warning did Samuel give to the Israelites about monarchical rule? Be specific.
10. How did Saul displease God so much that it cost Saul his crown?
11. What was the final service God asked Samuel to perform? Why did it trouble Samuel?

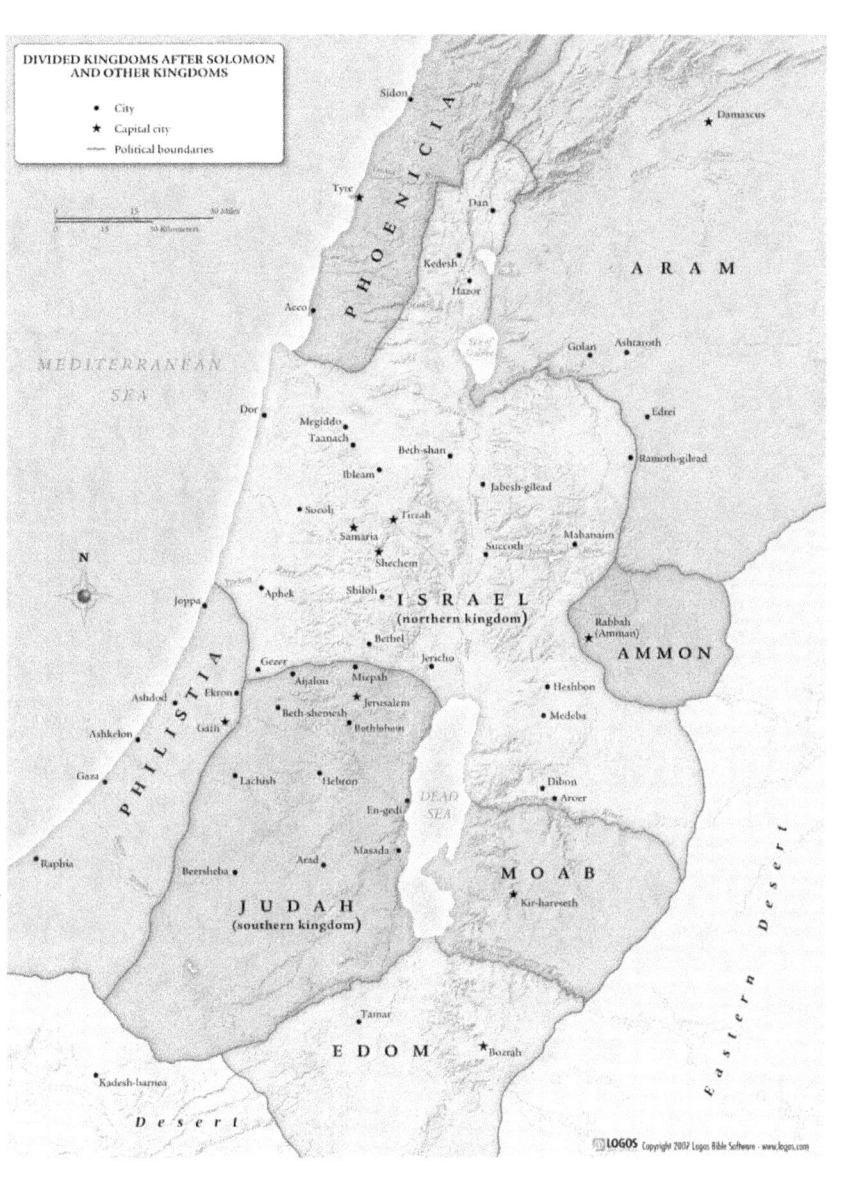

Chapter Three
NATHAN

"You are that man!"

The so-called *Age of Kings*, encompassing the reigns of Saul, David and Solomon, was not an era that featured a high volume of prophets. After Samuel's efforts paved the way for monarchical rule after approximately 220 years of the preceding "Age of Judges" (1250-1030 BCE), the only other prophet of stature was Nathan, whose career extended from the reign of King David into that of his successor, his son Solomon.

Nathan's prophetic ministry is memorable primarily as a result of two conversations between Nathan and King David.

Nathan apparently served King David as an advisor, and it was in this capacity that he made his first Scriptural appearance (2 Samuel 7:2) when David lamented to him that he himself lived in a home constructed of cedar while the Lord's Ark of the Covenant was kept in a humble tent. After Nathan urged David to take whatever steps he saw fit to provide the Lord with a more appropriate dwelling place because "the Lord is with you," it was later that night that Nathan, in a dream, encountered God who countermanded his earlier advice with the words:

> *Go and tell My servant David… "You are not the one to build a temple for Me to live in…I have never lived in a temple; I have traveled around living in a tent." (2 Samuel 7:5-6)*

But God's message to David continued with words that filled him with joy and pride.

> *I will make one of your sons king and will keep his kingdom strong. He will be the one to build a temple for Me, and I will make sure that his dynasty continues forever. (2 Samuel 7:12-13)*

When David heard these words through the prophet Nathan, Nathan's calling as a prophet of the Lord was established, even though it lacked the other elements of the "call narrative." David entered the presence of God in the tent of the Ark and expressed both his gratitude to the

Lord and his acknowledgement of his own unworthiness to receive such a blessing. Of course, David was unaware at this time of the pain and heartache that would soon fill his life as a result of the poor choices he was about to make.

Before the next dramatic example of Nathan's prophetic ministry can be placed in its proper perspective, it should be noted that David, in conformity with the social mores and customs of his time and culture, embraced the polygamy that was practiced throughout his society.

David's first wife, Michal, was betrothed to him by her father King Saul, although Saul later reneged on this marriage and gave her to a different husband. Eventually Michal returned to David - but bore him no children.

During his seven years as king of Hebron, before his reign extended to Judah, David took another six wives, each of whom bore him a son. Ahinoam bore Amnon, David's firstborn son, Abigail gave birth to Kil'av, Maachah bore Absolon, Haggith bore Adoniyya, Abital gave birth to Shefatya, and Eglah bore David's sixth son, Yitre'am. Although the names of the women are listed nowhere, Scripture reports that:

> After moving from Hebron to Jerusalem, David took more concubines and wives, and had more sons and daughters...Ibhar, Elishua, Nepheg, Japhia, Elishama, Eliada and Eliphelet." (2 Samuel 5:13-15)

The importance of chronicling the multiple wives and children of King David lies in establishing the fact that David already had a dynamic and multifaceted family life with personal, romantic and sexual relationships that should have fulfilled him in many ways and on many levels. For this reason, the circumstances surrounding David's next personal relationship are less than understandable - and much less acceptable.

BATHSHEBA

The sordid tale begins when David awoke from an afternoon nap and climbed to the palace roof for a breath of fresh air. From that vantage point, he spied a beautiful woman bathing in a nearby dwelling - and lusted after her. After learning that her name was Bathsheba and that she was married to Uriah the Hittite, one of the officers in David's army, David called her to the palace, where they had sexual relations leading to Bathsheba's pregnancy. To cover his tracks, David summoned Uriah to Jerusalem from the military campaign against the Ammonites in which he was fighting in the hope that his return to Bathsheba would lead him to believe that her unborn child was his. However, Uriah chose to uphold a military code of honor that required sexual abstinence while on a military campaign (to promote self-discipline and focus), and thus kept his distance from his wife.

So David compounded his indiscretion with yet another even more grievous sin. He instructed his general, Joab, to place Uriah in the front line on the Ammonite battlefield to increase the likelihood of his death. This ploy was perversely successful as Uriah was killed in battle, and David took Bathsheba as his wife, wrongly believing his duplicity had gone undetected. He was wrong. Sin of any kind is nothing that can be concealed from God - and the Lord was decidedly displeased with David's transgressions.

The Lord sent Nathan to confront David, and Nathan did so by relating a story to him:

> ...There were two men who lived in the same town; one was rich and the other poor. The rich man had many cattle and sheep, while the poor man had only one lamb, which he had bought. He took care of it, and it grew up in his home with his children. He would feed it some of his own food, let it drink from his cup, and hold it in his lap. The lamb was like a daughter to him. One day a visitor arrived at the rich man's home. The rich man didn't want to kill one of his own animals to fix a meal for him; instead, he took the poor man's lamb and prepared a meal for his guest. (2 Samuel 12:1-4)

When David expressed his outrage at the greed of the rich man, declaring:

> ...*the man who did this ought to die! For having done such a cruel thing, he must pay back four times as much as he took.* (2 Samuel 12:5-6)

Nathan's response:

> *You are that man!* (2 Samuel 12:7)

shocked him to the core, as he came to realize that nothing escapes God's notice. But it was God's punishment that devastated David all the more:

> *Now, in every generation some of your descendants will die a violent death because you have disobeyed me and have taken Uriah's wife. I swear to you that I will cause someone from your own family to bring trouble on you. You will see it when I take your wives from you and give them to another man; and he will have intercourse with them in broad daylight. You have sinned in secret, but I will make this happen in broad daylight for all Israel to see.*
>
> (2 Samuel 12:10-12)

So David would be forced to experience firsthand the consequences of his own sins - infidelity, betrayal and the death of members of his family. Nathan also told him:

> *The Lord forgives you; you will not die. But...your child will die.* (2 Samuel 12:13-14)

And so it came to pass that after Bathsheba gave birth to David's son, the child died within seven days, the result of a brief illness. Bathsheba later gave birth to David's other sons Shimea, Shobab, Nathan (not the prophet!) and Solomon (also known as Jedidiah), but the other aspects of David's punishment, as foretold in Nathan's prophecy, unfolded dramatically over the course of years.

First, David's son Amnon raped his half-sister Tamar. This enraged Absalom, Tamar's brother, who then killed Amnon. Years later, Absalom rebelled against his father David and declared himself king.

After forcing David to flee Jerusalem, he publicly had intercourse with ten of David's concubines who remained behind in Jerusalem. Absalom, in turn, was killed in battle by David's general, Joab, despite David's request that his troops spare Absalom's life. Although Absalom's usurpation was treachery, David grieved for his son nevertheless. In David's later years, he saw his son Adonijah also declare himself to be king, and it was this action that brought the prophet Nathan to the forefront one final time.

David promised Bathsheba that her son Solomon would succeed him as king, so he sent Nathan and the priest Zadok to anoint Solomon as his heir. The members of David's court then paid their respects to Solomon, wishing him a successful reign. Upon his accession, Solomon killed Adonijah and the priest (Abiathar) and army general (Joab) who supported his claim to the throne, essentially ending the violence that was foretold in Nathan's prophecy about God's punishment of David for his sins. Beside his unnamed infant son by Bathsheba, David also suffered the deaths of his sons Amnon, Absalom and Adonijah (the fourfold punishment that was demanded of David (*he must pay back four times as much as he took*) as well as the public humiliation of ten of his concubines (*he will have intercourse with them in broad daylight*). The cycle of retribution had come to its conclusion.

Little is known of the last days of Nathan. As a tutor of the young Solomon and as a trusted advisor of both Kings David and Solomon, it is assumed that Nathan offered much needed advice to Solomon when he began construction of the Temple in Jerusalem, but there are no further Biblical references to him. Nathan's major contributions to the monarchy include his prediction that Solomon would be the architect of the Temple, that David would experience both punishment and forgiveness by God for his sins, and his assistance in steering succession of David away from Adonijah and toward Solomon. The rest, as they say, is history.

CHAPTER 3: QUESTIONS FOR REVIEW

1. Who was the king of Israel when Nathan began his prophetic ministry?
2. What advice did Nathan first give the king that later had to be reversed?
3. Why was the king pleased with this reversal?
4. What was the indiscretion committed by the king that incurred the wrath of God?
5. How did the king makes matters worse by compounding his indiscretion?
6. What was the significance of Nathan's story that ended with the words "You are that man?"
7. What are the names of all of the king's wives?
8. How was the king punished for his sins?
9. What promise did the king make to Bathsheba?

PROPHETS OF THE DIVIDED KINGDOM

Chapter Four
ELIJAH

"O Lord my God, restore this child to life!"

The Father of the Prophets. That's an awful big nickname for a fella to live up to! And yet, that is a longstanding designation reserved for Elijah, who seemingly came out of nowhere to turn Israelite society on its head.

The prophet Elijah, whose ministry extends approximately from 870-845 BCE is certainly one of the most dramatic figures in the Old Testament, and his story unfolds not unlike that of our own culture's Lone Ranger. But it is impossible to fully appreciate his ministry and accomplishments without an least a "bare bones" understanding of the time and society in which he lived.

After Solomon ascended to the throne in Israel, little is heard of the prophet Nathan who championed and anointed him. It is believed that he continued in an advisory capacity to King Solomon, but no further word in Scripture heralds his ministry. Nor is his death chronicled, either. What we DO know is that Solomon's reign gradually evolved into one of tyranny, as Solomon both heavily conscripted and taxed his subjects to expand his realm and to support his many construction projects.

Upon the death of Solomon and subsequent succession of his son Rehoboam around 930 BCE, the people asked their new king for relief from the heavy taxes and workload imposed on them by Solomon. Counseled by his friends not to show weakness, Rehoboam refused - threatening to impose even stiffer taxes and labors on his subjects. This rash and politically suicidal decision resulted in a schism leading ten tribes to secede from Rehoboam's rule. They formed the kingdom of Israel (also known as Samaria) to the north, and left Rehoboam to rule his now much smaller kingdom - Judah - to the south. They selected Jeroboam, who spearheaded their secession, as their king.

At this point, priority attention must be paid to the northern kingdom of Israel, for the next few prophets of importance (beginning with Elijah) will be directing their ministries northward. And the reason for this is quite understandable. Under Jeroboam and his successors (Nadab, Baasha, Elah, Zimri, Omni - and especially Ahab) the practice of idolatry, as well as other heinous violations of the covenant made between Abraham and Yahweh, became more and more pronounced. This set the stage for a queue of prophets to encourage the Israelites to return to the Covenant as well as to admonish them for their transgressions.

UNSTABLE AND IMMORAL LEADERSHIP

Monarchs are supposed to provide leadership not only politically, but morally, as well. And in Israel (and Judah, too) that moral leadership began and ended with conformity to the Abraham-Yahweh Covenant. So when Jeroboam constructed several temples featuring golden calf icons in Bethel and Dan, a downward spiral orchestrated by the king had begun. Jeroboam's temples were built to discourage his subjects from journeying south to Jerusalem in the "other" kingdom of Judah to worship there. He also named priests who were not of the tribe of Levi - strike two! But the die for other violations of the Covenant had been cast.

Jeroboam's son Nadab succeeded him, but Nadab and his entire family were assassinated by Baasha, a captain in his army. Baasha was, in turn, succeeded by his son Elah, who was likewise assassinated by a chariot commander named Zimri, who assumed the crown. Zimri committed suicide shortly thereafter when the army elected Omri as king. So it seems that monarchical benignity was clearly in short supply.

Omni was hailed as a powerful "warrior king" whose exploits are chronicled in the historical records of other civilizations besides Israel - such as those of the Moabites and Assyrians - even though scant mention is made of him in the Hebrew Scriptures. The Old Testament is much more effusive in its praise of a morally upright ruler than in that ruler's political or military accomplishments, so Omri is barely mentioned at all. But it was his son Ahab who took center stage as the epitome of abrogation of the Abraham-Yahweh Covenant. Ahab married a Phoenician princess named Jezebel, an ardent worshipper - perhaps even a priestess - of the god Baal and goddess Asherah. Many of the tribes who lived in close proximity to Israel paid allegiance to Baal as a god of fertility - the god responsible for sending the rain that nourished the crops and kept the soil fertile. Asherah was also worshipped as a goddess of fertility. Jezebel exerted enormous influence over Ahab and convinced him to join her in the worship of Baal. An even greater offense was her manipulation of Ahab to construct temples to Baal and designate the worship of Baal as the "state religion" of Israel. These violations of the Covenant - which mandated that the people of Israel must worship Yahweh alone - were beyond abject, and needed to be addressed.

And all of this led to Elijah. There is no record of a "call narrative" that directed Elijah down the path of prophethood. All that is known of him is that he was a Tishbite - a resident of the town of Tishbe in the region of Gilead. According to 1 Kings 17:1, Elijah simply appeared before King Ahab and informed him that he spoke for Yahweh, the true God who controls the weather, and announced a coming drought (*...there will be no dew or rain for the next two or three years until I say so.*) that would demonstrate Yahweh's power. Ahab was nonplussed, but Elijah promptly disappeared - escaping the clutches of Ahab before he could be questioned and detained - or worse.

Elijah, under Yahweh's direction, fled east of the Jordan River to a place called Cherith Brook, where he was given a supply of freshwater and where the Lord sent ravens to bring him bread and meat for nourishment. Eventually, when the continuing drought caused the brook to dry up, the Lord directed Elijah to journey to the town of Zarephath (somewhere between the Phoenician cities of Tyre and Sidon), where a widow had been entrusted by God to care for him.

It was here that Elijah performed the first of the miracles attributed to him. When he encountered the widow (whose name is not recorded in Scripture), he asked her to bring him water and bread. But the woman's poverty was profound, and she had reached the end of her food supply.

All I have is a handful of flour in a bowl and a bit of olive oil in a jar. I came here...to prepare what little I have for my son and me. That will be our last meal, and then we will starve to death. (1 Kings 17:12)

But Elijah assured her:

...the God of Israel says, "The bowl will not run out of flour nor the jar run out of oil before the day that I...send rain." (1 Kings 17:14)

Truer words were never spoken. As Elijah had promised, the widow's supply of flour and oil remained replenished for many days (the exact time frame is unknown) but, eventually, tragedy struck. The widow's young son took ill, unable to catch his breath, and died. The widow held Elijah responsible.

Man of God, why did you do this to me?" (1 Kings 17:18)

Elijah himself was confused by this unexpected turn of events, unaware that this tragedy was actually setting the stage for his second miracle. He took the child to the upstairs room where he had been staying, laid him on the bed, and began to pray.

O Lord, my God, restore this child to life! (1 Kings 17:21)

The Lord heard Elijah's prayer, and the boy began to breathe again. When Elijah returned him to his mother, she exclaimed,

Now I know that you are a man of God and that the Lord really speaks through you! (1 Kings 17:24)

While this is not supported by evidence or testimony anywhere in the Old Testament, the *Zohar*, a book of Jewish mysticism, identifies this child raised from death by Elijah as Habakkuk, one of the Minor Prophets whose writings appear in later sections of the Hebrew Scriptures. However, insofar as Elijah lived in the ninth century BCE while

Habakkuk dates from the seventh century BCE, this identification is highly unlikely.

When the drought entered its third year, the Lord instructed Elijah to present himself to King Ahab as a prelude to the ending of the drought. He approached Obadiah, a trusted servant of King Ahab, and asked him to inform the king of his return to Israel. But Obadiah balked at this, afraid that Elijah would again disappear and Ahab's wrath would fall on him. After Elijah reassured Obadiah, a meeting of the two was arranged and accusations began to fly back and forth. Ahab began with the words:

> *So there you are - the worst troublemaker in Israel! (1 Kings 18:17)*

to which Elijah responded

> *I'm not the troublemaker. You are - you and your father. You are disobeying the Lord's commands and worshipping the idols of Baal. (1 Kings 18:18)*

Elijah was determined to demonstrate once and for all that Ahab, Jezebel and the people of Israel had all misplaced their trust in Yahweh in favor of Baal and Asherah. He instructed Ahab to summon the people of Israel as well as the priests of Baal and Asherah to Mount Carmel, a 1700-foot mountain near the west coast of Israel, thought to be a sacred place. Ahab agreed. That set the stage for one of the most dramatic confrontations recorded in the annals of the Old Testament - a contest between Elijah (representing Yahweh) and the 450 priests of Baal - to determine which god was worthy of the worship of the Israelites.

SHOWDOWN ON MOUNT CARMEL

After challenging the Israelites to choose between Yahweh and Baal, but receiving nothing more than stony silence as a reply, Elijah proposed a contest: he and the priests of Baal would prepare two sacrificial bulls for immolation and construct altars for the sacrifices - but they would not light fires. Rather, they would call upon their gods to send the fire, and the god who "delivered the goods" would prove to be the true God of the Israelites.

Elijah graciously allowed the priests of Baal to go first. They prayed to Baal for hours, beseeching him to send the fire to immolate the sacrificial bull. Eventually, Elijah began to make sport of their efforts.

> *Pray louder! He is a god! Maybe he is daydreaming or relieving himself, or perhaps he's gone off on a trip! Or maybe he's sleeping, and you've got to wake him up! (1 Kings 18:27)*

The priests of Baal chanted louder, but after several more hours had elapsed, their efforts remained fruitless. The scene then shifted to Elijah. In addition to constructing an altar with 12 stones that represented the twelve tribes of Israel, he took additional steps to dramatize the power of Yahweh. Elijah dug a trench around his altar and ordered 12 jugs of water to be poured over the bull and the wood beneath it. The water not only drenched the bull, but flooded the trench encircling the altar. This saturation would make it that much more difficult to sustain a fire.

Elijah approached the altar and began to pray:

> *O Lord, the God of Abraham, Isaac and Jacob, prove now that You are the God of Israel and that I am Your servant and have done all this at Your command. Answer me, Lord, answer me, so that this people will know that You, the Lord, are God and that You are bringing them back to yourself. (1 Kings 18:36-37)*

Immediately fire came down from heaven to completely incinerate all that had been drenched - the bull, the wood and the altar - as well as scorching the earth and evaporating the water in the trench. Upon seeing this, the people prostrated themselves, proclaiming

> *The Lord is God; the Lord alone is God! (1 Kings 18:39)*

Elijah ordered that the priests of Baal should be seized, and they were all put to death.

As dramatic as this encounter was, the saga was brought to completion when Elijah informed Ahab that the drought was about to end and he should return to his palace in Jezreel before the rains prevented him from doing so. Within a short time, the sky was filled with dark clouds and a heavy rain erupted. Elijah ran ahead of Ahab's chariot all the way to Jezreel.

When Ahab arrived in Jezreel, he informed his wife Jezebel of the result of the contest on Mount Carmel as well as the killing of the 450 priests of Baal. One might think that an important lesson would have been learned by Ahab and Jezebel as a result of this dramatic show of force by Yahweh - but some lessons seemingly go unlearned. Not only was no gratitude displayed by Ahab and Jezebel to the God who ended the drought, not only did they fail to grasp both the supreme power of Yahweh and the utter failure of Baal and his priests, but Jezebel immediately set out to kill Elijah, who was forced to flee for his life. Arriving first in the southern village of Beersheba in the Negev Desert, Elijah was instructed by an angel to travel to Mount Sinai, where Elijah encountered God. Instructed to ascend to the top of the mountain, Elijah awaited God. First, a furious wind began to howl, but the Lord was not in the wind. It was followed by an equally thunderous earthquake, but the Lord was not in the earthquake. After the earthquake had subsided, a fire erupted, but the Lord - again - was not in the fire. Finally, Elijah heard the soft whispering of a voice, and this was the manner in which the Lord chose to address Elijah.

Atop Mount Sinai, the Lord issued a series of instructions to Elijah:

> *Return to... Damascus...and anoint Hazael as king of Syria...Jehu...as king of Israel...and...Elisha...to succeed you as prophet. Anyone who escapes being put to death by Hazael will be killed by Jehu, and anyone who escapes Jehu will be killed by Elisha. (1 Kings 19:15-17)*

Elijah set out to accomplish these tasks. After finding Elisha in his village of Abel-meholah and placing his cloak on Elisha's shoulders, he designated him as his prophetic "heir apparent" - and Elisha remained with him from that moment.

NABOTH'S VINEYARD

Unfortunately, the atrocities perpetrated by Ahab and Jezebel continued to mount, and Elijah's dealings with the monarchs were still ongoing. The next royal misadventure (and Elijah's response to it) involved a vineyard owned by a poor man named Naboth in close proximity to Ahab's palace in Jezreel. The saga began innocently enough. Ahab wanted to purchase the vineyard owned by Naboth to convert it into a vegetable garden. He offered to provide Naboth with a different, comparable vineyard or purchase the vineyard from him at a fair price. Nothing untoward as of yet. But when Naboth refused to part with a tract of land that had been owned by his family for a number of generations, Ahab reacted emotionally, vacillating between anger and depression.

When Jezebel questioned him, Ahab explained Naboth's refusal to sell, and Jezebel asked him:

> *Well, are you the king, or aren't you? Get out of bed, cheer up, and eat. I will get you Naboth's vineyard!* (1 Kings 21:7)

Jezebel resorted to unscrupulous means to secure the vineyard - and it is unknown whether Ahab was aware of her underhandedness or not. She used Ahab's royal seal to concoct a scenario where Naboth could be publicly (and wrongly) accused of cursing both God and the king - grounds for immediate stoning to death. Her plan went off without a hitch, and upon Naboth's death, Jezebel urged Ahab to take possession of the vineyard he coveted - an opportunity at which he jumped. But God, of course, sees all things, and He instructed Elijah to address Ahab in much the same way he instructed Nathan to address David (about his murder of Uriah) generations earlier.

When Elijah confronted Ahab in Naboth's garden, their verbal sparring began anew. Ahab asked:

> *Have you caught up with me, my enemy?* (1 Kings 21:20)

to which Elijah responded:

> Yes I have. You have devoted yourself completely to doing what is wrong in the Lord's sight. So the Lord says to you "I will bring disaster on you. I will do away with you and get rid of every male in your family, young and old alike....
>
> And concerning Jezebel...dogs will eat her body in the city of Jezreel. Any of your relatives who die in the city will be eaten by dogs, and any who die in the open country will be eaten by vultures." (1 Kings 21:20-24)

Elijah's pronouncement had a profound impact on Ahab, who ripped his royal robes and donned sackcloth as a sign of contrition for his sins. Upon seeing this act of humility, the Lord relented, and chose not to bring calamity upon the house of Ahab while Ahab lived, but to mete His punishment on the family of Ahab in the next generation.

It was approximately two years after Ahab's act of humility and contrition before the Lord that Ahab made the decision to attack the town of Ramoth in Gilead - a town that the Syrians (also known as Aramaeans) had annexed from Israel and inhabited. Ahab invited Jehoshaphat, the king of Judah, to join him in this campaign - and he consulted a number of prophets - not including Elijah - to predict his likelihood of victory. However, despite an affirmative response from these prophets, Ahab was killed in battle by a stray arrow that pierced the joint in his armor - and his reign was brought to an end. He was succeeded by his son Ahaziah, who failed to learn any lessons whatsoever from the atrocities committed by his parents. Ahaziah

> sinned against the Lord, following the wicked example of his father Ahab, his mother Jezebel, and King Jeroboam, who had led Israel into sin. He worshipped and served Baal, and...aroused the anger of the Lord... (1 Kings 22:52-53)

Ahaziah's reign lasted but two years. Upon his ascension, he was immediately confronted with two crises - first, an insurrection from the Moabites, a tribe to the southeast of Israel along the eastern shore of the Dead Sea, and second, a fall from the balcony of his palace that left him seriously incapacitated and bedridden. Curious as to the length of his recovery, he sent emissaries to the Philistine city of Ekron to consult its patron god, Baalzebub. But it was this action that brought about the involvement of Elijah. An angel of the Lord instructed Elijah to intercept these emissaries and return them to Ahaziah to answer the question:

> *Why are you going to consult Baalzebub, the god of Ekron? Is it because you think there is no god in Israel? You will not recover from your injuries; you will die!* (2 Kings 1:6)

Upon discovering that this interceptor was none other than Elijah, Ahaziah sent troops to capture and bring Elijah before him. But fire came down from heaven on two separate occasions to destroy the troops. The third time troops arrived to arrest Elijah, the angel instructed Elijah to return with them without fear. Elijah repeated the message that Ahaziah would die, and this prophecy came true. Since Ahaziah had no sons to succeed him, the throne passed to his brother Joram.

ELIJAH'S NON-DEATH

The time had now arrived for Elijah's duties as prophet of the Lord to come to an end. Elijah and his assistant Elisha traveled extensively from Bethel in the north to Jericho in the south, ultimately arriving at the River Jordan, where Elijah rolled up his cloak, struck the water, and crossed to the other side with Elisha on dry ground - in much the same way as Moses led his people across the Red Sea in the Exodus from Egypt. When Elijah asked Elisha what he could do for him before being taken away, Elisha responded:

> *Let me receive the share of your power that will make me your successor. That is a difficult request to grant, Elijah replied. 'But you will receive it if you see me as I am being taken away from you; if you don't see me, you won't receive it.* (2 Kings 2:9-10).

Suddenly a chariot of fire, pulled by horses of fire, came between them and carried Elijah off in a whirlwind. Elisha witnessed this, cried, rent his garment (a gesture of loss and anguish), picked up Elijah's cloak, and struck the water with it as Elijah had done earlier to create a path of dry land, and crossed to the other side. Fifty other prophets who were witnesses to these events acknowledged that Elisha had been imbued with the same power granted to Elijah, and had been chosen to continue his prophetic ministry. These other prophets opted to search for Elijah for the next three days - despite Elisha's protests that their efforts would be futile - but neither they nor Elisha ever saw Elijah again.

So Biblical tradition maintains that Elijah is one of the very few human beings mentioned in Scripture who never died. That's not something you see every day! He has historically been viewed as the one who will herald the arrival of the Messiah, which explains why many who lived at the time of Christ identified John the Baptist as Elijah. The New Testament also presents the Transfiguration of Jesus on the mountain (possibly either Mount Tabor, Mount Panium, Mount Hermon or Mount Nebo) as a moment when Jesus - in the presence of His Apostles - conversed with both Moses and Elijah. And Elijah, throughout the ages, has also played a prominent role in the Seder meal that celebrates Passover. After grace before the meal is intoned, a cup of wine is poured for Elijah - and the front door is opened to welcome him. The open door is symbolic of trust in God's protection - a trust that was clearly evident in the lifestyle of Elijah - and the cup of wine (which is not consumed) represents the coming redemption which will be announced by Elijah - but isn't here yet (which explains why the wine isn't yet enjoyed!)

Elijah is one of the truly towering figures of the Old Testament - and a paradigm of loyalty, obedience, trust and faith. He's called the "father of the prophets" for good reason indeed.

CHAPTER 4: QUESTIONS FOR REVIEW

1. What prediction was made by Elijah to King Ahab? What occurrence made this prediction necessary?
2. Approximately when did Elijah live - and in what kingdom did he preach?
3. What is the significance of Queen Jezebel in the story of Elijah's life and ministry?
4. What two miracles were performed by Elijah in Zarephath?
5. What event of dramatic and theological significance took place on Mount Carmel?
6. In what manner did God speak to Elijah at Mount Sinai? What assignments did Elijah receive from God?
7. What was the nature of the relationship between Elijah and Elisha?
8. Why was Naboth's vineyard an important part of Elijah's ministry? How did the vineyard bring about a transformation in King Ahab?
9. Did King Ahaziah treat God more respectfully and with greater devotion than his father Ahab? Did Ahaziah have a more cordial relationship with Elijah?
10. How did Elijah's ministry come to an end? Why do we say that Elijah never died?

Chapter Five
ELISHA

"His flesh became firm and healthy, like that of a child"

The prophetic mission and message of Elisha is first introduced in the story of his mentor Elijah. These two prophets are probably discussed more in relation to each other than any other two prophets named in the Old Testament. There are no other examples of a prophet "passing along" his ministerial responsibilities in such a manner as this. It's much the same as when one member of a track relay team passes his baton to the next runner in his unit or the World Wrestling Federation sponsors a "tag team" wrestling match.

Elisha is first introduced when Elijah is issued a series of instructions from the Lord, one of which was to journey to Syria to anoint Elisha to succeed him as prophet (as mentioned in the previous chapter: see 1 Kings 19:15). Elisha was the son of Shaphat, a wealthy landowner from the town of Abel-meholah near the River Jordan. Elijah discovered Elisha ploughing his field with twelve pair of oxen, and symbolically placed his mantle on Elisha's shoulders. Understanding the meaning of this gesture, Elisha slaughtered the oxen to feed his people, kissed his parents good-bye, and followed Elijah. He proceeded to reject his previous life as a farmer to embrace his prophetic call in much the same way as Peter and Andrew left behind their lives as fishermen to follow Jesus.

The prophetic call of Elisha began in the First Book of Kings, but his ministry really commenced in 2 Kings. The time arrived for Elijah to be taken up to heaven, but nowhere in Scripture is it mentioned how Elijah and Elisha had become aware of this. They were on the road leaving Gilgal, when Elijah asked Elisha to stay behind, as the Lord had ordered him to go to Bethel. Elisha refused to leave him, and they both proceeded first to Bethel, then to Jericho, then to the River Jordan. It was at the River Jordan that Elijah struck the waters with his cloak and parted them to cross to the other side - reminiscent of Moses parting the waters of the Red Sea in the Exodus event. Elijah asked Elisha:

Tell me what you want me to do for you before I am taken away. (2 Kings 1:9)

Elisha asked to receive a double portion of Elijah's prophetic power in order to succeed him, but Elijah was unsure if this was a blessing that was within his authority to bestow. He replied:

> *That is a difficult request to grant...but you will receive it if you see me as I am being taken away from you... (2 Kings 1:10)*

When a fiery chariot pulled by fiery horses suddenly appeared between them and carried Elijah to heaven in a whirlwind, Elijah bore witness to this amazing spectacle. He cried out in anguish, tore his garments in grief, and picked up Elijah's mantle. He struck the water with it, and the waters receded to create a pathway of dry land upon which Elisha walked to the other side. He was greeted by fifty "guild prophets" - prophets who chose to live together in community and prophesied while in some form of ecstatic, music and dance-fueled trances - who acknowledged his primacy as successor to Elijah. And so, Elisha's prophetic ministry began. Elisha served in this capacity for approximately 60 years (892-832 BCE), during the reign of Kings Joram, Jehu, Jehoahaz and Jehoash.

A STUDY IN CONTRAST

While Elijah's ministry was largely characterized by condemnation of idolatry and other atrocities emanating from the royal court of Ahab and Jezebel, the ministry of Elisha - with several exceptions - demonstrated a more genteel brushstroke - healing and compassionate in substance, but also characterized by a series of predictions as well as activities with great political consequences. Of course, it should always be noted that any miraculous acts or accurate predictions made by any of the prophets ultimately came from the power that God bestowed upon them - and not through powers of their own creation.

The scriptural passages in the First and Second Books of Kings offer a startling and comprehensive contrast between Elijah and Elisha, emphasizing that the differences between the two - despite their very complementary and consecutive ministries - existed on so many different levels. For example, Elijah had long hair while Elisha was teased for his baldness; Elijah suddenly appeared and disappeared out of and into the wilderness, while Elisha's life was more settled. Elijah made predictions while Elisha performed miracles of healing, yet Elijah's "non-death" was miraculous while Elisha's death was ordinary. Elijah was more of a firebrand and rabble-rouser, while Elisha had a gentler and more sympathetic disposition. While the hallmark of Elijah's ministry was condemnatory, Elisha focused on God's mercy. Elijah was frequently at odds with the reigning monarchs, while Elisha befriended monarchs. Elijah was more of a solitary figure while Elisha enjoyed the company of others.

Elisha's first act in his prophetic ministry was to purify the drinking water in the city of Jericho, where water pollution was held responsible for multiple deaths and miscarriages. Having received a request for aid from representatives of the city, Elisha poured salt into the spring from which the water flowed and intoned a prayer:

> *This is what the Lord says: "I will make the water pure, and it will not cause any more deaths or miscarriages." (2 Kings 2:21)*

Elisha restored the purity of the water - saving perhaps countless lives. The water thus restored has been free of pollution to this day.

A second miraculous act of kindness opens chapter 4 of 2 Kings. Elisha encountered the widow of a guild prophet who was unable to pay her late husband's debt to a creditor. The creditor, in turn, wanted to take the widow's two sons to serve as slaves until the debt was repaid through their servitude. When the widow informed Elisha than she had few assets - just a small jar of olive oil - he instructed her to borrow as many empty jars and containers from her neighbors as possible, and fill these with the oil from her own small jar. The oil flowed long enough to fill all of the borrowed vessels. Elisha told her to

> *...sell the olive oil and pay all your debts, and there will be enough money left over for you and your sons to live on. (2 Kings 4:7)*

This act of mercy was closely followed by another prediction and miraculous healing - also involving another woman who had shown kindness to Elisha. In the city of Shunem, Elisha met a wealthy couple who invited him to dine with them. Eventually, after frequent trips to Shunem, Elisha was gratified to see that his benefactors had now prepared a small furnished room for him to use whenever he visited their city. Elisha wanted to repay their kindness, but they were not in need of any favors. Elisha's servant, a man named Gehazi, mentioned that the couple had no children - and the husband was now aged. Elisha told the woman:

> By this time next year you will be holding a son in your arms. (2 Kings 4:16)

Elisha's prediction held true, and a son was born within the following year. But tragedy struck several years later when the boy collapsed in pain while helping his father and his father's servants at harvest time. The boy was rushed to his mother's side, but he died within the next few hours. His mother lay him on the bed in Elisha's room - and set out to find him.

The woman knew that Elisha was at Mount Carmel, so she hurried there and told him what happened.

Elisha sent his servant Gehazi ahead, telling him to hold Elisha's walking stick over the boy until he and the boy's mother arrived. When Elisha reached Shunem, Gehazi told him that the boy had not revived.

> Elisha...went alone into the room and saw the boy lying dead on the bed. He closed the door and prayed to the Lord. Then he lay down on top of the boy, placing his mouth, eyes and hands on the boy's mouth, eyes and hands...the boy's body started to get warm. Elisha got up, walked around the room, and then went back and again stretched himself over the boy. The boy sneezed... and then opened his eyes. (2 Kings 4:32-35)

When the boy's mother arrived, she prostrated herself at Elisha's feet, with her face touching the floor.

On another occasion, while Elisha was instructing an assemblage of guild prophets, one of his servants prepared a stew with gourds that were tainted. Realizing they had been inadvertently poisoned, the prophets cried out for help.

> Elisha asked for some meal, threw it into the pot, and said, "Pour out some more stew for them." And then there was nothing wrong with it. (2 Kings 4:41).

And shortly thereafter, again while meeting with guild prophets, Elisha was presented with twenty loaves of barley from a patron from Baal Shalishah. He instructed his attendant to distribute the loaves among the 100 guild prophets, but the attendant expressed doubt that the loaves could feed such a large number.

> Elisha replied, "Give it to them to eat, because the Lord says that they will eat and still have some left over." (2 Kings 4:43)

And all were sufficiently fed, and there was food left over. Of course, this miracle is a clear precursor to the New Testament story of Jesus feeding the five thousand men (along with women and children), as recorded in all four Gospel accounts (Matthew 14:13-21, Mark 6:30-44, Luke 9:10-17 and John 6:1-14).

NAAMAN THE LEPER

Probably the most renowned instance of Elisha's healing ministry is his cure of Naaman's leprosy. Naaman was a general in the Syrian army - and a worshipper of the Syrian god Rimmon. He was also a leper - and how unusual that a man with such a dreaded affliction should be given such responsibilities and held in such high regard by his king and people. The Syrians had defeated Israel in battle under Naaman's leadership, and among the captured "spoils of war" was a young Israelite girl who became the slave of Naaman's wife. Either because she had become fond of Naaman's family during her servitude or, in the hope of currying favor with the family, she suggested to Naaman's wife:

> *I wish that my master could go to the prophet who lives in Samaria! He would cure him of his disease. (2 Kings 5:3)*

Upon hearing this, Naaman brought this before his king, Ben-Hadad II, who wrote him a letter of introduction to present to Joram, the king of Israel. When Naaman arrived in the court of King Joram and presented the letter, the king read it with confusion and anger, thinking that King Ben-Hadad II was attempting to pick a fight with him. He tore his garments as a sign of futility and despair.

Upon hearing of the king's distress, Elisha sent word to direct Naaman to Elisha's own dwelling to

> *...show him that there is a prophet in Israel. (2 Kings 5:8)*

Naaman and his servants, carrying an assortment of expensive gifts, arrived at Elisha's home, but Elisha did not greet him. Instead, he sent a servant to instruct Naaman to wash himself seven times in the River Jordan to be cured of his leprosy. Naaman was angered by this response, feeling slighted at what he considered to be shabby treatment, even making disparaging comments about the quality of the river itself. His servants intervened and persuaded him to do as Elisha had requested. Naaman capitulated and, after washing himself seven times in the Jordan, was completely healed.

> *His flesh became firm and healthy, like that of a child. (2 Kings 14)*

Naaman, now experiencing an "attitude adjustment," returned to Elisha's home with gratitude and a newfound faith in the Lord. He offered gifts to Elisha - quantities of gold, silver and fine clothing - but Elisha refused such gratuities - and Naaman set out to return to his home in Syria, with the intention of worshiping only the God of Israel.

The story of Naaman's cure should end here - but it doesn't. Elisha's servant Gehazi was dismayed that Elisha would not accept tribute from Naaman, so he followed Naaman's retinue and caught up with them. Gehazi lied to Naaman that Elisha had changed his mind and was now requesting a quantity of silver and fine clothing for two of the guild prophets who were visiting him. Naaman was quite pleased to comply, and Gehazi brought these gifts to his own home. When Elisha asked Gehazi where he had gone and Gehazi lied to him as well, Elisha replied,

> *Wasn't I there in spirit when the man got out of his chariot to meet you? This is no time to accept money and clothes...Now Naaman's disease will come upon you, and you and your descendants will have it forever! (2 Kings 5:26-27)*

Clearly, the lesson here is that the same power that God has given to His prophets to cure can also be used to inflict - when the circumstances demand it.

The next significant moment in Elisha's ministry involved a prediction that Elisha was reluctant to deliver. When Ahab's death put his son Ahaziah on the throne of Israel, Ahaziah's reign was less atrocity-filled than that of his father, but only minimally so. Upon his brother Joram's ascendancy to the throne, he faced a rebellion from King Mesha of Moab, who had previously paid an annual tribute to his father Ahab. Joram decided to launch an attack on Moab, but not before enlisting the aid of King Jehoshaphat of Judah and the (unnamed) King of Edom. When these three kings set out to begin their campaign, within a week they had exhausted their supply of water while marching through the wilderness of Edom - and were now at the mercy of their rebellious adversary. The kings wanted to consult the Lord through one of his prophets, and they requested assistance from Elisha, who was traveling with them. Initially, Elisha refused to help Joram, for whom he had little respect, but ultimately agreed as a token of deference to King Jehoshaphat of Judah, a morally upright monarch whom he held in esteem. Elisha instructed the kings to dig a series of ditches in a dry river bed near their encampment, and promised that they would be filled with enough water to satisfy themselves, their troops and their pack animals. He also predicted a complete victory over the Moabites - as well as the destruction of all of the Moabite cities and the ruination of their springs and planting fields. And this victory came to pass just as Elisha had said. (2 Kings 3)

POLITICAL INTERVENTION

Several of Elisha's other accomplishments involved the ongoing tension between Israel and Syria, also known as Aram. At one point, the King of Syria attempted to ambush the King of Israel, but Elisha was able to warn him in time to avert the plot. This foreknowledge of Syria's plans enabled Elisha to warn the king on several other occasions as well, and the Syrian king began to think that one of his close advisors was a traitor. He asked them:

> Which one of you is on the side of the king of Israel? (2 Kings 6:11)

When his advisors informed him that

> The prophet Elisha tells the king of Israel what you say, even in the privacy of your own room (2 Kings 6:12)

the king demanded that Elisha be found and captured. When Elisha was discovered in the town of Dothan, the Syrian army - with horses and chariots - encircled the town overnight to take him into custody. Elisha then prayed to the Lord to blind the Syrian soldiers, and the Lord honored this request. Elisha then approached the sightless Syrian militia and informed them that they had come to the wrong town, but that he would lead them to the man they sought. They agreed, and Elisha led them to the city of Samaria, the capital of Israel.

Upon arriving in Samaria, Elisha petitioned the Lord to restore their sight, and the soldiers realized instantly that they had been deceived and victimized and were now at the mercy of Israel. Elisha instructed the king of Israel not to kill the Syrian invaders, but rather to feed them and return them to their homeland. This act of mercy taught the Syrian army and its king of the power of the God of Israel - and marked the end of further attempts to raid Israel - at least, for a time.

Despite this show of God's mercy and power, King Ben-Hadad II of Syria eventually reversed direction and sent troops to lay siege to Samaria, the capital of Israel. As the siege continued and the food shortage in Samaria worsened, some desperate citizens of Samaria resorted to eating their own children. King Joram of Israel wanted to hold Elisha responsible for this crisis, and sent a messenger to retrieve him for execution. Elisha foresaw this, and told the king's messenger upon his arrival that the food shortage would be over within the next day. When the messenger expressed his doubt, Elisha told him that the food would be available, but he would not eat of it. Meanwhile, the Lord had confused the Syrian troops into thinking that a large mercenary army of Hittites and Egyptians had been hired by the Samaritans to rout them. They fled in haste, leaving most of their supplies and food behind them - which the Samaritans were only too happy to plunder. But, in the act of racing to the abandoned Syrian camp to retrieve the food, the Samaritan crowds trampled the king's messenger to death. So Elisha's prophecy came true - the food was available by the next day, and the king's messenger did not share in it.

Another instance of the veracity of Elisha's predictions can be found during a trip that Elisha took some time later to Damascus, the capital of Syria. When King Ben-Hadad II of Syria, who was ill, heard that Elisha was visiting his city, he summoned his servant Hazael to bring a gift to Elisha and ask him if he would recover from his illness. Elisha's response to Hazael was confusing.

> *The Lord has revealed to me that he will die; but go to him and tell him that he will recover. (2 Kings 8:10)*

Elisha then stared at Hazael for a long time and burst into tears. When Hazael asked him why he was weeping, Elisha's response was chilling.

> *Because I know the horrible things you will do against the people of Israel...You will set their fortresses on fire, slaughter their finest young men,*

batter their children to death, and rip open their pregnant women. (2 Kings 8:12)

When Hazael told Elisha that, as a servant, he didn't have the power to do such things, Elisha told him that God had revealed to him that Hazael would become king of Syria. (Recall that the Lord had asked Elijah to anoint Hazael as king of Syria in 1 Kings 19:15). Hazael returned to Ben-Hadad and delivered Elisha's false message of his recovery, and then suffocated the king with a wet blanket to ascend to the throne himself. As king, Hazael waged war against both King Joram of Israel and Joram's nephew, King Ahaziah of Judah. Hazael's victory at Ramoth-Gilead gave him control over Israelite territory east of the River Jordan, expanding his influence, wealth and power. It was also at this battle that King Joram was severely wounded and forced to return to the city of Jezreel, with Ahaziah accompanying him.

Elisha sent one of the young guild prophets who were allegiant to him to the city of Ramoth-Gilead to anoint Jehu, one of Joram's army officers, as the next king. In keeping with God's instructions to Elijah in 1 Kings 19:15-17, the prophet told Jehu:

The Lord, the God of Israel, proclaims, "I anoint you king of My people Israel. You are to kill your master the king, that son of Ahab, so that I may punish Jezebel for murdering My prophets and My other servants. All of Ahab's family and descendants are to die; I will get rid of every male in his family, young and old alike. I will treat his family as I did the families of King Jeroboam and of King Baasha of Israel. Jezebel will not be buried; her body will be eaten by dogs in the territory of Jezreel." (2 Kings 9:6-10)

Jehu journeyed to Jezreel where King Joram asked him if he had come in peace. Jehu replied that there could be no peace due to the idolatry that had been observed throughout Israel. Joram attempted to escape via chariot, but Jehu killed him with an arrow and dumped his body in the field that Ahab and Jezebel had stolen from Naboth (see 1 Kings 21). He also killed King Ahaziah of Judah, as he attempted to flee as well. Ahaziah, who was also of the house of Ahab (his mother Athalia was Ahab's daughter), had similarly introduced the same idolatry that had plagued Israel into the southern kingdom of Judah. Jehu returned to Jezreel, where he had Jezebel thrown from her palace window into the street, where her remains were scavenged by feral dogs, thus fulfilling Elijah's prophecy of her demise.

Jehu's destruction of the house of Ahab was completed in Samaria, the capital of Israel, when the leading citizens of Samaria vowed allegiance to Jehu and beheaded the remaining seventy descendants of Ahab's family. This completed the Lord's promise to exact vengeance on Ahab and Jezebel for their idolatry by eliminating their progeny. As Jehu journeyed from Jezreel to Samaria, he encountered other relatives of Ahaziah whom he also put to death, and, upon his arrival in Samaria, he took steps to kill all the remaining worshippers of Baal in that city. Pretending to offer a great sacrifice to Baal in the temple devoted to him, Jehu summoned all Baal worshippers together - but had them executed. The temple of Baal he converted into a latrine. However, despite Jehu's attempts to obliterate the worship of Baal in Israel, he made the mistake of following King Jeroboam's practice of worshipping golden bull idols in Dan and Bethel. Some lessons never seem to be learned!

Jehu, who ruled Israel from 841-814 BCE, was succeeded by his son Jehoahaz, who continued to permit the same idolatry that was tolerated by his father Jehu. He, in turn, was succeeded by his son Jehoash, who likewise retained the same idolatrous practices of his forefathers. It was during the reign of Jehoash that Elisha took ill and died.

There are numerous other stories chronicled in the Hebrew Scriptures about Elisha's miracles and predictions (miraculously recovering a borrowed ax handle from the waters of the Jordan, predicting an upcoming famine, restoring a man to life whose remains touched Elisha's remains), but it is not necessary to record every mention of Elisha in the Bible to recognize his unique qualities of unwavering faith in God, compassion to those in need of healing, and dedication to commitment to the Abraham-Yahweh Covenant.

There's just one other episode in the life of Elisha that is worth mentioning only insofar as it seems so inconsistent with the rest of his ministry. Shortly after purifying the drinking water of Jericho, Scripture records a troubling altercation on the road to Bethel.

> *Elisha left Jericho...and on the way some boys came out of a town and made fun of him. "Get out of here, baldy!," they shouted. Elisha turned around, glared at them and cursed them in the name of the Lord. Then two she-bears came out of the woods and tore forty-two of the boys to pieces. (2 Kings 2:23-24)*

Certainly such an extreme, violent response to a rather lightweight, inconsequential insult resonates as inconsistent with Elisha's ministry of compassion. In *First and Second Kings* of the New Collegeville Bible Commentary series (2012), Professor Alice L. Laffey of Holy Cross College equated this story with the account in the Gospel of Mark (Mark 11:12-14) where a hungry Jesus curses a fig tree for bearing no fruit, even though the tree was out of season. Her conclusion is that the behavior of both Jesus and Elisha, while totally out of character for both, emphasizes that those who have been entrusted with power from God are not to be treated contemptuously, whether accidentally or purposefully. Certainly this provides a great deal of food for thought.

CHAPTER 5: QUESTIONS FOR REVIEW

1. For how long did Elisha serve as a prophet? During what years? Under which monarchies?
2. Compare and contrast the ministry "styles" of Elijah and Elisha.
3. What are three examples of miracles performed by Elisha that were of special benefit to women?
4. Why did Naaman have both positive and negative feelings about Elisha? Where does the servant Gehazi fit into this story?
5. How did Elisha aid the three kings in Edom?
6. What happened at the incident in Dothan? How did it forestall an invasion of Israel?
7. How did Elisha's ability to foretell the future affect King Ben-Hadad II of Syria and his servant Hazael?
8. What responsibilities were entrusted by God to Jehu upon his anointing as king?
9. Were Jehu's son and grandson loyal to Yahweh? Explain.
10. What was the unexpected result of insulting Elisha's hairline?

Chapter Six
AMOS

"Let justice flow like a stream and righteousness like a river…"

t. Paul, in addressing the community of believers at Corinth, reminded the members of the church that:

there are different kinds of spiritual gifts, but the same Spirit gives them. There are different ways of serving, but the same Lord is served. (1 Corinthians 12:4-5)

Long before Paul wrote these words, a similar sentiment enveloped the ministries of the Old Testament prophets, who were also inspired by the same Spirit - yet conveyed His words through many different and unique styles of preaching, writing, prognostication, behavior and personal lifestyle.

Amos was called to a prophetic ministry that differed from that of his predecessors. Elijah and Elisha fulfilled their ministries to the people of the northern kingdom of Israel (or Samaria) as residents of that Israelite nation. But God's Chosen People had already split into two separate kingdoms upon the death of King Solomon in 931 BCE - the southern kingdom of Judah ruled by Solomon's oppressive son Rehoboam, and the larger, secessionist northern kingdom of Israel ruled by Jeroboam. While both kingdoms shared a common language, culture, heritage and faith as the Chosen People of Yahweh, there were sufficient disparities and disagreements between them to create an authentic enmity - with only occasional forays into a tepid alliance. It was into this climate of mutual mistrust and division that Amos was thrust into service.

THREE STRIKES

Amos was called by God to minister to the people of Israel while he himself was born and bred in the southern kingdom of Judah - in the small village of Tekoa. This was "strike one" against him - being sent to preach to a population that didn't know him, and viewed him as an outsider and rabble rouser. But add to that "strike two" against Amos - he had no social status to aid him as a platform from which he could credibly deliver God's messages to Israel. Poor social standing similarly hampered his predecessor Elijah, and would be a bane to future prophets such as Jeremiah, as well.

Ancient Israel was divided along class lines - royalty and the landed aristocracy comprised the "haves" while the peasants, peddlers and herders were the "have nots." Throw into the mix the *anawim* - the poorest of the poor, the outcasts and the otherwise marginalized members of Israelite society - and the resulting melange was a self-divided society. Amos arrived on the scene as both a shepherd and a dresser of sycamore fig trees, essentially a poor laborer whose message held no weight whatsoever. This was the unwelcome task and "Mission Impossible" entrusted to Amos - to deliver a message to a people who were more likely to "kill the messenger" than heed his words.

We know nothing of the "prophetic call" of Amos. How was he first approached by the Lord? How did he respond? Did he require reassurance from God? These are questions to which Scripture provides no answers. But there is one thing we DO know - Amos considered himself to be a true prophet - one whose authenticity derived from selection by God - as opposed to the "fabricated" prophetic tradition emanating from training schools such as were attended by the guild prophets of that era.

The "third strike" against Amos was the economic climate of Israel at the time of Amos' arrival. Under King Jeroboam II, Israel had waged a series of successful military campaigns against the Syrians (or Aramaeans), Ammonites and Moabites which greatly expanded the size and the wealth of Israel. Life was good, trade was booming, money was plentiful and the nation was presently at peace. What was the point in listening to anything this lower class outsider had to say?

The entirety of Amos' ministry (760-753 BCE) unfolded during the reign of Jeroboam II, but his words play a pre-eminent role in the chronicles of Scripture insofar as he is the first prophet whose message was recorded in writing. We know very little of Amos' trafficking with the people of Israel. Virtually nothing related to his personal relationship with the Israelites or his actions upon arriving in Israel are revealed in Scripture. Just about everything we know of Amos flows from his words - and his words express a profundity of emotion that hadn't been expressed before quite so vociferously.

Unlike Elijah's utter condemnation of idolatry and Elisha's miracles of compassion and "political" predictions, the primary messages Amos wished to convey were those of social justice and sincerity of heart. While Israel was experiencing a "golden age" of peace and prosperity, its blessings and benefits were being enjoyed only by the affluent - with no thought of assistance to the less fortunate. In truth, many of the other Canaanite tribes who lived in close proximity to Israel viewed wealth as a gift of the gods to their favorite devotees, and poverty as a plague befalling a lower class who deserved no better treatment. Therefore, offering assistance to the lowly wasn't viewed as selfishness, but rather as a way of pleasing the gods who would have viewed generosity to the unfortunate as a violation of their expressed wishes. The upper classes of Israel were only all too willing to adopt this self-aggrandizing, hoarding philosophy.

SEVEN CONDEMNATIONS

The book of Amos takes a slightly circuitous route in its eventual condemnation of Israel. It begins with a series of denunciations made by the Lord - with concomitant punishments - against seven of Israel's neighbors, including Judah - before targeting Israel itself.

To Syria (also called Aram), the Lord censured its cruelty to the people of Gilead, and promised destruction of its royal palace, fortresses and the city gates of its capital city of Damascus - and the eventual imprisonment of its people in the land of Kir. (Amos 1:3-5)

Philistia was condemned for its enslavement and sale of individuals to the people of Edom. Its punishment would be the burning of its capital city of Gaza and its fortresses, the removal of the rulers of its major cities of Ashdod, Ashkelon and Ekron, and the death of the remaining Philistine population. (Amos 1:6-8)

The people of Tyre were denounced for exiling large numbers of people to Edom as well as violating a friendship treaty. Therefore, their city walls and fortresses would also be burned down. (Amos 1:9-10)

The Edomites were the descendants of Jacob's brother Esau, and the Edomites were merciless in their mistreatment of the Israelites, their relatives. So the Lord promised to burn their city of Teman and the fortresses of Borzah. (Amos 1:11-12)

The Lord accused the Ammonites, in their thirst for more territory, of "ripping open pregnant women in Gilead." The penalty for that included the burning of the city walls of Rabbah, the chief city of Ammon, and the exile of its king and military officers. (Amos 1:13-15)

The people of Moab desecrated the remains of the king of Edom by burning his bones to ashes - purely out of hate and vindictiveness - and the Lord's punishment would result in the burning of the Moabite fortress at Kerioth and the killing of the Moabite people and their king. (Amos 2:1-3)

Although God had sent Amos from his homeland in Judah to deliver His message in Israel, Amos' homeland was not spared either. The Lord condemned Judah for its failure to keep His commands and for its return to the idolatrous ways of its ancestors. Therefore, Judah's fortresses would also be burned down.

Except for Judah, whose crimes and sins were internal, the other Canaanite tribes were facing the retribution of the Lord as a result of their "external" sins against one another. In his 1962 classic *The Prophets*, Professor Abraham J. Heschel of New York's Jewish Theological Seminary explained the moral foundation of the charges levied against them: "...The nations were not, like Israel, condemned for internal transgressions, but for international crimes, although there was no law in existence governing international relations. Amos...presupposes the conception of a law which was not embodied in a contract, the conception of right and wrong which precedes every contract, since all contracts derive their validity from it. Hence a conception of law was expressed which is binding for all men, though it was not formally proclaimed; and there was a Lawgiver capable of enforcing it and coercing transgressors."

This blanket condemnation of Judah and the other local Canaanite tribes reflects an understanding that God is not only the Deity of the Israelites who holds His "Chosen People" to a high standard of fidelity, justice and mercy - but can and does expect this same level of cultural and social ethics from all of the tribes He has created.

JUDGMENT AGAINST ISRAEL

God's final judgment, as presented by Amos, was reserved for Israel itself. Israel was condemned for a litany of sins worthy of God's punishment. As the Lord articulated to Amos:

> *They sell into slavery honest men...they trample down the weak and helpless...a man and his father have intercourse with the same slave girl...at every place of worship men sleep on clothing that they have taken from the poor as security...at temple they drink wine which they have taken from those who owe them money. (Amos 2:6-8)*

But the condemnation did not end there:

> *The Lord says, "These people fill their mansions with things taken by crime and violence. They don't even know how to be honest...You women of Samaria who grow fat like the well-fed cows of Bashan...mistreat the weak, oppress the poor, and demand that your husbands keep you supplied with liquor." (Amos 3:10, 4:1)*

> *You have oppressed the poor and robbed them of their grain...You persecute good men, take bribes, and prevent the poor from getting justice in the courts. (Amos 5:11-12)*

And again:

> *How terrible it will be for you that stretch out on your luxurious couches, feasting on veal and lamb!...You drink wine by the bowlful and use the finest perfumes, but you do not mourn over the ruin of Israel. (Amos 6:4-6)*

Amos' condemnation of Israel was radically different from Elijah's condemnation one century earlier. Here the issue is not one of Covenant violation through idolatry, but rather through greed and decadence. Their infidelity did not come through devotion to other deities - but to themselves, at the expense of the less fortunate. When they were condemned for eating veal and lamb and drinking wine to excess, their transgressions went beyond simple selfishness. They were flaunting their wealth and opulent lifestyle in the faces of the poor and downtrodden. And beyond that, they were of the mindset that they could find favor with God, not through a generosity of spirit to the anawim, but rather through participation in the rituals and sacrifices that were thought to placate a narcissistic Deity.

The Israelites were prioritizing the superficial over the essential. Their attitude was one of "we can commit whatever atrocities against the less fortunate that suit us - and pay for our so-called 'sins' through the appropriate sacrifice, grain offering or song of contrition" rather than reflecting on their much deeper responsibility through the Covenant to offer the necessary assistance to the poor to meet their needs and improve their living conditions. In fact, their weekly Sabbath day was viewed as a nuisance that interfered with their profit-making atrocities.

> *You say to yourselves, "We can hardly wait for the holydays to be over so that we can sell our grain. When will the Sabbath end, so that we can start selling again? Then we can overcharge, use false measures, and fix the scales to cheat our customers. We can sell worthless wheat at a high price. We'll find a poor man who can't pay his debts...and we'll buy him as a slave." (Amos 8:5-6)*

This was the barren philosophy of the Israelites that motivated Amos' most passionate and most virulent pronouncement against the superficiality of ritual:

The Lord says, "I hate your religious festivals; I cannot stand them! When you bring me burnt offerings and grain offerings, I will not accept them; I will not accept the animals you have fattened to bring me as offerings. Stop your noisy songs; I do not want to listen to your harps. Instead, let justice flow like a stream, and righteousness like a river that never runs dry." (Amos 5:21-24)

DIRE CONSEQUENCES

How will Israel be punished for its sins against the poor and its self-absorption and decadence? Through the writings of Amos, God's punishments are articulated often and in a vast variety of forms:

Now I will crush you to the ground, and you will groan like a cart loaded with grain. (Amos 2:13)

I will destroy winter houses and summer houses. The houses decorated with ivory will fall in ruins; every large house will be destroyed. (Amos 3:15)

The days will come when they will drag you away with hooks; every one of you will be like a fish on a hook. You will be dragged to the nearest break in the wall and thrown out. (Amos 4:2)

There will be wailing and cries of sorrow in the city streets...There will be wailing in all the vineyards. (Amos 5:16-17)

You will be the first to go into exile. Your feasts and banquets will come to an end. (Amos 6:7)

I hate the pride of the people of Israel....I will give their capital city and everything in it to the enemy. (Amos 6:8)

I am going to send a foreign army to occupy your country. It will oppress you from Hamath Pass in the north to the Brook of the Arabah in the south. (Amos 6:14)

I, the Sovereign Lord, am watching this sinful kingdom of Israel, and I will destroy it from the face of the earth. But I will not destroy all the descendants of Jacob. (Amos 9:8)

The reason why Amos was forced to put his message in writing - and why he is considered the first of the so-called Writing Prophets - is the reaction of Amaziah, the high priest at the shrine of Bethel, to a series of visions Amos received from God that showed the means by which God would punish Israel for its sins - visions of locusts and fire consuming Israel.

> *In my vision I saw...locusts eat up every green thing in the land (Amos 7:2)*

and

> *I saw [the Sovereign Lord] preparing to punish his people with fire. The fire burned up the great ocean under the earth and started to burn up the land... The holy places of Israel will be left in ruins. I will bring the dynasty of King Jeroboam to an end. (Amos 7:4,9)*

Amaziah reported to King Jeroboam II that Amos' speeches were inflammatory and treasonous, and ordered Amos to leave Israel. Amos complied, but not before issuing a dire prophesy against Amaziah:

> *And so, Amaziah, the Lord says to you, "Your wife will become a prostitute in the city, and your children will be killed in war. Your land will be divided up and given to others, and you yourself will die in a heathen country. And the people of Israel will certainly be taken away from their own land in exile." (Amos 7:17)*

Amos chronicled all of his pronouncements, predictions, accusations, preachings and visions in order that his message would reach its intended audience - Israel - even if he were not physically present to proclaim it. To this day, Amos is often referred to as "the prophet of social justice," whose words and images continue to resonate as a result of the passion with which he delivered God's message to Israel. Unlike Teddy Roosevelt who suggested one should "speak softly but carry a big stick," Amos - a "lion of God" - roared!

CHAPTER 6: QUESTIONS FOR REVIEW

1. To whom did Amos deliver God's message?
2. How did Amos' message differ from the message of Elijah?
3. What was Amos' background - his career, his homeland, etc.
4. Why was Amos' target audience unwilling to listen to him? (3 reasons)
5. How did the philosophy of the other Canaanite tribes about the poor influence the wealthy people of Israel?
6. Why did Amos offer condemnations against the people of Syria, Philistia and Tyre? How did he say God would punish them?
7. In what ways did Amos say God intended to punish Israel?
8. What was God's reaction to the religious rituals and sacrifices employed by the people of Israel?
9. What were the circumstances that led to Amos' expulsion from Israel?
10. What nickname is often given to Amos because of his strong belief about the importance of compassion toward the poor?

Chapter Seven
HOSEA

"...the people of Israel are not My people and I am not their God"

One of the most interesting contrasts between the Old and New Testaments is their vastly different understandings of the nature of God Himself. Throughout the Old Testament, God is usually viewed as a "Warrior King" - regal and authoritarian - who will protect His people in battle and help them to defeat their enemies, but will not hesitate to discipline or punish His subjects if they should fail Him. Failure, of course, would be judged by their conformity (or lack thereof) to the stipulations of the Yahweh-Abraham Covenant. God was quick to judge, quick to anger, quick to punish - and, both directly and indirectly, He caused a great deal of suffering, destruction and death.

By contrast, the God of the New Testament, as presented to the people of Judah by Jesus, was anything but a "Warrior King." God was a loving Father, whom Jesus called "Abba" - a term of endearment and intimacy that is more properly translated as "dad" than as "father." God is quick to understand, quick to forgive failings - and quick to love. Very different mindsets, indeed!

Part of the uniqueness of the ministry and message of Hosea is his attempt to straddle these two images of God in a way that displays the seriousness with which God treats violations of His Covenant with His Chosen People (via punishment) and the limitless nature of His love for His Chosen People (via forgiveness and restitution). He portrays a God who can serve as both a stern judge and a doting parent at one and the same time.

MINISTRY IN TURBULENT TIMES

Hosea arrived on the scene as a prophet to the northern kingdom of Israel just as the prophetic mission of Amos drew to its conclusion. Hosea's ministry extended for four decades throughout a politically turbulent time in the history of Israel - from the tail end of the reign of King Jeroboam II through the reigns of Zechariah, Shallum (who assassinated Zechariah), Menahem (who assassinated Shallum), Pekahiah (Menahem's son), Pekah (who assassinated Pekahiah) and Hoshea (who assassinated Pekah). In addition to this "in house" violence, bloodshed, intrigue and uncertainty, the rise of the brutal Assyrian Empire also engendered tremendous fear and unrest among the people of Israel, which also led the Israelites and their rulers into the worship of other gods and/or the establishment of (hopefully) protective political alliances, rather that placing their trust in the Lord.

Hosea's ministry, while immediately following the ministry of Amos, was quite different in its message and method. Where Amos condemned the Israelites and their leaders for their opulent lifestyle and utter disregard for the poor and disenfranchised, Hosea's message echoed that of his predecessor Elijah in his attacks on the idolatry practiced by the Israelites. Stephen M. Miller, in his 1998 text *Getting Into the Bible: Journey Through the Greatest Story of All Time*, concluded that "...the story of Hosea isn't mainly about spiritual rebellion or divine punishment. It's about God's inexplicable, relentless love even for people who treat Him like the enemy. For those who think the Old Testament God is cruel, Hosea reveals a preview of God practicing the compassion that His Son would later preach: 'Love your enemies.'"

MARRIAGE AND CHILDREN AS TOOLS OF MINISTRY

Another major difference between the ministries of Amos and Hosea was the medium of their messages. Amos journeyed from Judah to Israel to deliver his message - and made sure his words would reach their target audience by putting them in writing upon his expulsion. And while the words of Hosea were also transcribed, what made the ministry of Hosea unique among the Old Testament prophets was the pivotal role played by his immediate family in the conveyance of his message. In Hosea's case, as important as his words may have been, it was the events in his personal life that commanded center stage as his ministry to the people of Israel unfolded.

Hosea's personal background is rather sketchy. Theologian Abraham Heschel, in his 1962 text *The Prophets*, pointed out that "From his use of certain striking figures of speech it has been suggested that (Hosea) was a baker, lived as a farmer on the land, (and) was associated with the priesthood and the sanctuaries..." The opening line of the book of Hosea identifies the prophet as the son of Beeri, but offers no additional information on his early years. Similarly, nothing is articulated in Scripture about Hosea's "call narrative," the circumstances under which he was chosen by God to deliver His message.

So the story of Hosea's family life and its impact on his ministry and message is introduced in the first three chapters of the book of Hosea. It begins with an extremely unusual command from God to Hosea:

> *Go and get married; your wife will be unfaithful, and your children will be just like her. In the same way My people have left Me and become unfaithful. (Hosea 1:2)*

From the very beginning of Hosea's ministry, therefore, God is making it clear that Hosea's personal life, his marriage, and even his fatherhood will be used as dramatic metaphors to teach the people of Israel about the pain - and the consequences - of infidelity. As Hosea addressed his wife's unfaithfulness, so would the Lord address the unfaithfulness of Israel in abandoning the Lord for the worship of the Canaanite fertility god Baal.

Hosea married Gomer, the daughter of Diblaim, and it is unknown at what point after they were married that Gomer, as God had predicted, turned to prostitution. However, her infidelity was blatant; Hosea was a cuckold and everyone knew it. But despite her frequent acts of unfaithfulness, Hosea's love for his wife never flickered. He and Gomer had three children together, but God instructed Hosea to give specific names to their children as additional messages to Israel. Their first child, a son, was named "Jezreel," which was the city where Jehu assassinated the members of Ahab's royal family in 841 BCE (about 80 years earlier) and assumed the throne of Israel. The name Jezreel suggests that bloodshed and destruction are the price tags of unfaithfulness to the Lord and rejection of the Yahweh-Abraham Covenant. Ahab's descendants were slaughtered as a result of their worship of Baal rather than Yahweh.

The second child of Hosea and Gomer was a daughter, who was to be named "Lo-ruhama," which is translated either as "unloved" or "not to be pitied." In either event, God is making it clear that

> *I will no longer show love to the people of Israel or forgive them. (Hosea 1:6)*

This was a scathing indictment and "wake up call." And finally, their third child, a son, was named "Lo-ammi," meaning "not My people." This was the worst possible condemnation of Israel, expressing God's outright rejection of them.

> *Name him "Not-My-People," because the people of Israel are not My people, and I am not their God. (Hosea 1:9)*

MIXED MESSAGES

These three "warning shots" were designed to express to the Israelites the severity of their transgressions as well as the absolute necessity for a return to full fidelity to Yahweh. Yet, Hosea immediately reversed these dire warnings by speaking of the blessings that will flow from a loving and forgiving God who welcomes the return of His unfaithful ones.

> *The people of Israel will become like the sand of the sea, more than can be counted or measured. Now God says to them, "You are not My people," but the day is coming when He will say to them, "You are the children of the living God! The people of Judah and the people of Israel will be reunited. They will choose for themselves a single leader, and once again they will grow and prosper in their land. Yes, the day...will be a great day!"*
>
> *So call your fellow Israelites "God's People" and "Loved-by-the-Lord." (Hosea 1:10-2:1)*

Hosea's message read like a two-edged sword: on the one hand, unfaithfulness to Yahweh and the requirements of His Covenant were grave offenses that demanded retribution, but, on the other hand, a rejection of idolatry and return to the spirit of the Covenant would be rewarded with great blessings from a loving and forgiving God Who only wanted the best for His Chosen People.

Hosea used more of the same "tightrope walking" rhetoric in chapter two as he expressed both anger and love in equal measure. His words, while seemingly written to his children about their mother were, in reality, the metaphorical words of Yahweh directed to the idolatrous Israelites. First, the anger:

> *My children, plead with your mother - though she is no longer a wife to me, and I am no longer her husband. Plead with her to stop her adultery and prostitution.*
>
> *If she does not not, I will strip her as naked as she was on the day she was born.*
>
> *I will make her like a dry and barren land, and she will die of thirst. I will not show mercy to her children; they are the children of a shameless prostitute...I am going to fence her in with thorn bushes and build a wall to block her way. She will run after her lovers but will not catch them...At harvest time I will take back My gifts of grain and wine, and will take away the wool and the linen I gave her for clothing.*
>
> *I will strip her naked in front of her lovers, and no one will be able to save her from My power...I will destroy her grapevines and her fig trees, which she said her lovers gave her for serving them...I will punish her for the times that she forgot Me, when she burned incense to Baal and put on her jewelry to go chasing after her lovers.*
>
> *The Lord has spoken. (Hosea 2:2-13)*

But the anger, sparked by the pain of unfaithfulness, cannot upend the limitless love of the Lord:

> *...I am going to take her into the desert again; there I will win her back with words of love. I will give back to her the vineyards she had...I will make a covenant with all the wild animals and birds, so that they will not harm My people. I will also remove all weapons of war from the land, all swords and bows, and will let My people live in peace and safety. Israel, I will make you*

> My wife; I will be true and faithful; I will show you constant love and mercy and make you Mine forever. I will keep My promise...and you will acknowledge Me as Lord. At that time I will answer the prayers of My people Israel...I will establish My people in the land and make them prosper. I will show love to those who were called "Unloved" and to those who were called "Not-My-People." I will say, "You are My people," and they will answer "You are our God."(Hosea 2:14-23)

The above words delivered by Hosea - both those of censure and deliverance - were directed not to Gomer by her husband, but to the people of Israel by Yahweh. They symbolically outlined the consequences of infidelity as well as the benefits of faithfulness. But what of Hosea's personal life and the despair he must have felt as the result of Gomer's adultery? Insofar as God had chosen Hosea to serve as a dramatic metaphor for Himself - with Hosea's personal angst meant to mirror the pain that Israelite idolatry had caused God - Hosea's response to Gomer's unfaithfulness had to echo the mercy and forgiveness that Yahweh wished to offer to His Chosen People. So chapter three of Hosea - the last chapter to address Hosea's personal life - brings this metaphor to its conclusion.

> The Lord said to me, "Go again and show your love for a woman who is committing adultery with a lover. You must love her just as I still love the people of Israel, even though they turn to other gods..." (Hosea 3:1)

As a result of Gomer's adultery, either she willingly left Hosea to live with another man, or Hosea was forced to expel her from his house - which was the usual means of addressing adultery at the time. In either event, at the time God required Hosea to reach out to Gomer, she was living with another man who may have been serving as her procurer - what we would call in today's jargon a "pimp." Hosea could not merely invite her to return home; he had to pay for her as one would purchase a slave. Her price tag was

> fifteen pieces of silver and seven bushels of barley. (Hosea 3:2)

Upon Gomer's return, Hosea set down certain rules of behavior that Gomer was required to observe before their married life could return to "normal."

> *I told her that for a long time she would have to wait for me without being a prostitute or committing adultery; and during this time I would wait for her. (Hosea 3:3)*

It is with this injunction that the story of Hosea ends inconclusively. Did Hosea and Gomer live happily ever after? Did Gomer turn from her adulterous ways? Did Hosea welcome her back of his own volition - rather than under a mandate from the Lord? On a larger level, did the people of Israel recognize the parallel between Hosea and Gomer's relationship and the relationship between Yahweh and them? Did they understand the pain their infidelity has caused, yet recognized the Lord's infinite love and forgiveness in giving them another opportunity for reconciliation?

A LITANY OF ACCUSATIONS AND A FINAL PLEA

The Book of Hosea is fourteen relatively short chapters in length - which is why it is listed among the works of the Minor Prophets. Hosea's family life constitutes only the first three chapters, but it is within these chapters that the uniqueness of his ministry is dramatized. The remaining chapters of Hosea are best described as a series of accusations made by the Lord against the people of Israel for their transgressions against Him.

> *There is no faithfulness or love in the land, and the people do not acknowledge Me as God. They make promises and break them; they lie, murder, steal, and commit adultery. (Hosea 4:1-2)*

But the Lord ultimately holds the priests responsible for their lack of faith and devotion as well as for the poor example they set for the people.

> *My complaint is against you priests...You priests have refused to acknowledge Me and have rejected My teaching, and so I reject you...You grow rich from the sins of My people, and so you want them to sin more and more. (Hosea 4:4-8)*

Idolatry, of course, is center stage as a violation of the Yahweh-Abraham Covenant.

> *The people of Israel are under the spell of idols....After drinking much wine, they delight in their prostitution, preferring disgrace to honor. (Hosea 4:17-18)*

Because Israel was primarily an agricultural society, fertility of the soil was of paramount concern to most of the population. The Canaanite god Baal was worshipped as a fertility god, with rain thought to be the semen of Baal. The people believed that Baal could be encouraged to offer his semen (rain) to fertilize their fields if his devotees engaged in sexual intercourse with the priests, priestesses and prostitutes in his temples, hence the connection between idolatry and prostitution.

Chapter six addressed the people's insincere, half-hearted attempts at repentance and the high incidence of theft and murder - even at shrines and other sacred spaces. Chapter seven condemned the assassination of Israel's kings (four were murdered during the years of Hosea's ministry) as well as Israel's decision to place its trust in alliances with foreign powers such as Egypt and Assyria rather than with the Lord. Chapter eight returned to the issue of idolatry.

> *I hate the gold bull worshiped by the people of the city of Samaria. I am furious with them. How long will it be before they give up their idolatry? (Hosea 8:5)*

By chapter nine, the die had been cast and Hosea revealed over the next few chapters the consequences the people would face as a result of their infidelity to God.

> *Because of the evil they have done, I will drive them out of My land...They will become wanderers among the nations." (Hosea 9:15-17)*

Because you trusted in your chariots and in the large number of your soldiers, war will come to your people, and all your fortresses will be destroyed. (Hosea 10:13-14)

They refuse to return to Me, and so...Assyria will rule them. (Hosea 11:5)

In the final chapter, Hosea begged the people of Israel to change their ways. He pleaded:

Return to the Lord your God, people of Israel. You sin has made you stumble and fall. Return to the Lord, and let this prayer be your offering to Him: Forgive all our sins and accept our prayer, and we will praise You as we have promised.

Assyria can never save us, and war horses cannot protect us. We will never again say to our idols that they are our God. O Lord, You show mercy to those who have no one else to turn to. (Hosea 14:1-3)

And, one final time, God's message of forgiveness and restitution was resounded anew:

The Lord says, "I will bring My people back to Me. I will love them with all My heart; no longer am I angry with them...Once again they will live under My protection. They will grow crops of grain and be fruitful like a vineyard. They will be as famous as the wine of Lebanon. The people of Israel will have nothing more to do with idols; I will answer their prayers and take care of them. Like an evergreen tree I will shelter them; I am the source of all their blessings." (Hosea 14:4-8)

How tragic that Israel was unwilling to mend its ways and accept yet another opportunity to redeem itself and return to God's good graces. It was shortly after Hosea's ministry came to its end that his prediction came to fruition. In 721 BCE, Assyria attacked Israel and left it completely annihilated, repopulating its territory with foreigners. From this point, all eyes turned to the southern kingdom of Judah - all that remained of God's Chosen People.

Each of the prophets of the Old Testament shared a common ministry entrusted to them by Yahweh, who "called each by name." But each prophet also stands out for the uniqueness of his ministry and the media through which he chose to deliver God's message. Hosea is unlike the other prophets called by the Lord in that he was asked to make sacrifices different from those of the other prophets. Hosea was the only prophet called by God to suffer the emotional anguish caused by an unfaithful wife. The only prophet who faced ridicule and derision as a cuckolded husband. The only prophet whose family - wife and children - were part and parcel of his message. Other prophets, in truth, faced physical punishments and atrocities, but no other prophet was asked to endure the deeply personal angst faced by Hosea throughout his adult life. Perhaps only those who have been in a committed, loving relationship can truly fathom the depth of despair and humiliation that Hosea was asked to wear on his sleeve. Yes, God's call can be a very, very demanding one.

CHAPTER 7: QUESTIONS FOR REVIEW

1. How is the primary view of God found in the Old Testament different from the view of God found in the New Testament?
2. What was the political climate in Israel during the time that Hosea served as God's prophet?
3. Why were the people of Israel putting their trust in other gods and in political alliances with other tribes?
4. What is meant by the statement "Hosea and his relationship with his wife was a dramatic metaphor for God and the Israelites?"
5. What demand was placed on Hosea by God that was not required of any of the other prophets?
6. What is the prophetic significance of the names of Hosea's three children?
7. What information does Scripture provide about Hosea's background? His family? His career?
8. In what ways does Hosea say the Lord will punish Israel for its infidelity?
9. What did Hosea have to do to bring Gomer back into his household?

Chapter Eight

ISAIAH

"The people who walk in darkness have seen a great light"

The Bible records a number of instances of extreme old age among the men and women whose lives it chronicles. Methuselah lived to the ripe old age of 969 (Genesis 5:27), Adam was 930 years of age (Genesis 5:4), Seth, 912 (Genesis 5:8), Lamech, 777 (Genesis 5:31) and Eber, 464 (Genesis 11:16-17), just to name a few. Of course, exegetes are skeptical of the accuracy of these numbers, attributing them either to hyperbole or to an alternative method of temporal measurement. Therefore, the Book of Isaiah has proven itself to be rather enigmatic insofar as it spans approximately two and a half centuries of Biblical history - at least twice the maximum lifespan of even an incredibly healthy individual! Is it possible that one man was its author?

MULTIPLE ISAIAHS?

Biblical scholars clash mightily over the authorship of the Book of Isaiah. Many believe is was authored exclusively by one man, Isaiah of Jerusalem, while others point to differences in writing styles, topic areas and use of vocabulary to suggest that this book may have had two - or perhaps even three - different authors, or perhaps, schools of authors. For theologians who uphold this position, chapters 1-39 are believed to be the work of Isaiah of Jerusalem, while chapters 40-55 were composed by a different author (dubbed *Second Isaiah* or *Deutero-Isaiah*) and chapters 56-66 by yet a third writer (referred to as *Third Isaiah* or *Trito-Isaiah*). Since the second and third "supposed" authors or schools are unidentified - shrouded in mystery - it leaves Isaiah of Jerusalem as the sole historically identified author. While the debate over authorship continues to rage on, theologian J. Daniel Hays, in his 2010 text *The Message of the Prophets*, pointed out that both sides see a kind of unity in the book that is both theological as well as literary in its message and presentation.

What do we know about the prophet Isaiah? We know that he was the son of Amoz (not to be confused with the prophet Amos) and that he worked in the royal court of Judah as a historiographer. Most probably, he lived in Jerusalem. His ministry extended throughout the reign of four of Judah's kings: Uzziah, Jotham, Ahaz and Hezekiah, approximately from 742-687 BCE. We also know from his writings that Isaiah was a married man whose unnamed wife was simply referred to as "the prophetess." They had two sons, Shear-jashub (meaning "a remnant shall return") and Maher-Shalal-Hash-Baz (meaning "quick loot, fast plunder"), both names of which, as in the case of Hosea's three children, had predictive meanings. Michael Pennock's 1992 text *Discovering the Promise of the Old Testament* extolled the virtues of Isaiah of Jerusalem as a poet, a politician who was comfortable in the presence of the monarch and his courtly retinue and a spokesperson for God who wielded great prophetic power. Tradition holds that he was killed - brutally sawn in half - by the idolatrous King Manasseh, the son of Hezekiah, although there is no concrete proof to support this.

CALL NARRATIVE OF ISAIAH OF JERUSALEM

The call narrative of Isaiah unfolds as an exceedingly dramatic dream or vision experienced by Isaiah in the year King Uzziah died, circa 740 BCE:

> *...I saw the Lord. He was sitting on His throne, high and exalted...Around Him flaming creatures were standing, each of which had six wings. Each creature covered its face with two wings, and its body with two, and used the other two for flying. They were calling out to each other: "Holy, holy, holy! The Lord Almighty is holy! His glory fills the world."...I said, "There is no hope for me! I am doomed because every word that passes my lips is sinful, and I live among a people whose every word is sinful. And yet, with my own eyes I have seen the King, the Lord Almighty." Then one of the creatures flew down to me, carrying a burning coal...He touched my lips with the...coal and said, "...now your guilt is gone and your sins are forgiven." Then I heard the Lord say, "Whom shall I send? Who will be Our messenger?" I answered, "I will go! Send me!" (Isaiah 6:1-8)*

For Isaiah, this vision was transformative. Pat and David Alexander's 1999 *Zondervan Handbook to the Bible* suggests that Isaiah's call narrative vision profoundly and perpetually affected him as he experienced the full glory of God, the breadth and depth of human sin, and his newfound mission - once in receipt of the Lord's forgiveness - in the service of God. This had a profound impact on his ministry and his message of God's absolute love, mercy and righteousness.

With this mandate from the Lord, the prophetic ministry of Isaiah began. While it is important to know something of the personal lives of the prophets so their ministries can be placed in the proper historical and cultural context, they cannot be discussed or evaluated separately from the messages they were entrusted to convey by Yahweh. Whether the Book of Isaiah was composed by one author or is the combined work of several, its primary message can be divided into several component parts:

1. Chapters 1-39: a series of condemnations and predictions directed primarily to Judah, thought to be composed by Isaiah of Jerusalem
2. Chapters 40-55: words of encouragement to those Jews living in exile in Babylon, thought to be written by "Deutero-Isaiah" approximately 150 years after chapter 39
3. Chapters 56-66: promises of salvation and glory if those who have returned from exile in Babylon pursue righteous living, thought to be written by "Trito-Isaiah."

But it should also be remembered that the Book of Isaiah is much richer and more complicated than a simple threefold thematic division would indicate. Isaiah is thought to offer more predictions about the coming Messiah than any other book of the Old Testament. It is the single most-quoted book of Hebrew Scripture throughout the New Testament. And as the longest of the Prophetic Books of the Old Testament, it establishes Isaiah as perhaps the pre-eminent Major Prophet of Scripture.

ISAIAH OF JERUSALEM: CONDEMNATIONS AND PREDICTIONS

Isaiah began his ministry at a time of great political instability and turbulence. King Uzziah had just died, succeeded on the throne by his son Jotham, who had already been serving as co-regent due to his father's 8-year-long battle with leprosy. Because of Uzziah's military victories against the Philistines and Arabians, his organizational skills and development of agriculture, Judah was at the height of its power and wealth, but the Assyrian Empire under Tiglath-pileser III was a looming, external threat to attack and absorb both Judah and its neighbor to the north, Israel. Internally, Judah's affluence did not spare it from the pursuit of vice, and Jotham's reign was characterized by the continuing transgressions of idolatry, shallowness of faith and disregard for the poor by the wealthy. Isaiah necessarily had to address these abominations, and he did so in his first five chapters before even presenting in chapter six his call narrative qualifications as a God-appointed prophet.

Regarding the shallowness of faith, or perhaps "use of ritual as a substitute for authentic devotion" is more accurate, and its consequences for the poor, Isaiah wrote:

> Pay attention to what our God is teaching you. He says, "Do you think I want all these sacrifices you keep offering to Me? I've had more than enough of the sheep you burn as sacrifices and of the fat of your fine animals. I am tired of the blood of bulls and sheep and goats...I am disgusted with the smell of the incense you burn.
>
> I cannot stand your New Moon Festivals, your Sabbaths, and your religious gatherings; they are all corrupted by your sins...When you lift your hands in prayer, I will not look at you. No matter how much you pray, I will not listen, for your hands are covered with blood...Stop doing evil and learn to do right. See that justice is done - help those who are oppressed, give orphans their rights, and defend widows." (Isaiah 1:10-17)

The ongoing idolatry that infiltrated Judah from Israel continued to drive a wedge between Yahweh and His people. Isaiah wrote:

> The people follow foreign customs...Their land is full of idols, and they worship objects that they have made with their own hands...A day is coming when...the Lord Almighty will humble everyone who is...proud and conceited...Idols will

completely disappear, and the Lord alone will be exalted on that day." (Isaiah 2:6-7,11-12,18)

The opening chapters of Isaiah are also peppered with threats, as a result of these abominations.

But He will crush everyone who sins and rebels against Him; He will kill everyone who forsakes Him. (Isaiah 1:28)

Now the Lord...is about to take away from Jerusalem and Judah everything and everyone that the people depend on. He's going to take away their food and their water, their heroes and their soldiers, their judges and their prophets...their military and civilian leaders... (Isaiah 3:1-3)

Yes, Jerusalem is doomed! Judah is collapsing!...They sin as openly as the people of Sodom did. They are doomed, and they have brought it on themselves. (Isaiah 3:8-9)

These threats read as straightforward, damning prose. But chapter five of Isaiah also couches yet another threat in a more poetic form. Labeled the "Song of the Vineyard," Mary Reed Newland, in her 1999 text *Written on Our Hearts: The Old Testament Story of God's Love,* compared it with "a country music ballad telling of a broken-hearted lover lamenting betrayal by a faithless sweetheart":

Listen while I sing you this song, a song of my friend and his vineyard:

My friend had a vineyard on a very fertile hill.

He dug the soil and cleared it of stones; he planted the finest vines.

He built a tower to guard them, dug a pit for treading the grapes.

He waited for the grapes to ripen, but every grape was sour.

So now my friend says, "You people who live in Jerusalem and Judah, judge between my vineyard and me.

Is there anything I failed to do for it?

Why then did it produce sour grapes and not the good grapes I expected?

Here is what I am going to do with my vineyard:

I will take away the hedge around it, break down the walls that protect it, and let wild animals eat it and trample it down.

I will let it be overgrown with weeds. I will not trim the vines or hoe the ground; instead I will let briers and thorns cover it.

I will even forbid the clouds to let rain fall on it."

Israel is the vineyard of the Lord Almighty; the people of Judah are the vines He planted.

He expected them to do what was good, but instead they committed murder.

He expected them to do what was right, but their victims cried out for justice. (Isaiah 5:1-7)

So the Book of Isaiah wasted no time in addressing the sinfulness of the people of Judah - using words and imagery very understandable to all of them. But Isaiah's call narrative introduced him to the infinitude of God's forgiveness, and his opening condemnations and threats were also tempered with words of reconciliation and mercy.

Because the Lord is righteous, He will save Jerusalem and everyone there who repents. (Isaiah 1:27)

Righteous men will be happy, and things will go well for them. They will get to enjoy what they have worked for. (Isaiah 3:10)

By His power the Lord will judge and purify the nation and wash away the guilt of Jerusalem and the blood that has been shed there. (Isaiah 4:4)

Not unlike his contemporary Hosea, Isaiah preached both retribution for sin as well as mercy for repentance.

Isaiah's ministry unfolded in turbulent times, and much of the remainder of chapters 7-39 addressed this turbulence. With the

Assyrian Empire poised to attack, the kings of Syria (or Aram) and Israel (which Isaiah often refers to as "Ephraim") petitioned Jotham's successor Ahaz (not to be confused with Ahab, the wicked king of Israel one century earlier) to form a coalition with them against Assyria. When Ahaz refused to join them, Syria and Israel decided to attack Judah in the hope of killing Ahaz and replacing him with a different ruler who would choose to join them. This plot was known as the Syro-Ephraimite War, and Isaiah was sent by God to intervene.

Isaiah told Ahaz not to fear, but to place his trust in Yahweh and ask Yahweh to send a sign that all would be well.

> *If your faith is not enduring, you will not endure...Ask the Lord your God to give you a sign. (Isaiah 7:9-11)*

But Ahaz, who had already begun to "dabble" with idolatry, refused to do so, pretending that it would be presumptuous to make demands on God. Isaiah then offered him a sign from God anyway:

> *A young woman who is pregnant will have a son and will name him "Immanuel." By the time he is old enough to make his own decisions...the land of those two kings who terrify you will be deserted. (Isaiah 7:14-16)*

At the time Isaiah uttered these words, it was thought that "Immanuel" would be a future son to Ahaz - his successor Hezekiah - guaranteeing the continuation of the Davidic line to which he belonged. The people of Judah had not yet come to expect that God would send a Messiah to save them; it was not for many years that these words would be interpreted as a prophecy of a coming Savior.

Ahaz disregarded the words of Isaiah and chose to enter into an alliance with Assyria rather than place his trust in Yahweh. He again ignored a warning from Isaiah:

> *The Lord is going to bring on you, on your people, and on the whole royal family, days of trouble worse than any that have come since the kingdom of*

> Israel separated from Judah - he is going to bring the king of Assyria. (Isaiah 7:17)

Isaiah went on to compare Assyria's attack on Judah with killer bees overrunning the land and with a razor humiliating Judah by shaving the facial hair off its men. He predicted that Judah would be completely devastated, with its people struggling to find sufficient food, and its vineyards overrun with thorns and briers.

> The Lord said, "Assyria! I use Assyria like a club to punish those with whom I am angry. I send Assyria to attack a godless nation, people who have made me angry. I send them to loot and steal and trample the people like dirt in the streets." (Isaiah 10:5-6)

Admittedly, Ahaz's decision to ally himself with Assyria initially looked like a wise diplomatic move when Assyria assimilated Syria and Israel and spared Judah. But rather than view Judah simply as an ally, Tiglath-pileser III required Ahaz to swear allegiance to him, making Judah a vassal territory of Assyria. This was not a development that Ahaz expected. Neither was the annual tribute that Assyria expected Judah to pay to show its continued loyalty. But this was the scenario Ahaz was forced to play out. Isaiah's prophecy of Assyria's ascendancy proved to be true. So, hoping to win favor with Tiglath-pileser III, Ahaz swore homage to him and to the gods of Assyria and re-created one of the altars in Jerusalem to the gods of Assyria, replacing the altar to Yahweh and modifying worship services to accommodate it. He introduced astrology, and:

> he even sacrificed his own son as a burnt offering to idols [the Assyrian god Moloch]. (2 Kings 16:3)

Ahaz's rule was a complete disaster for Judah, especially so in its return to idolatry. Clearly, some lessons are only learned the hard way, and ignoring the words of authentic prophets like Isaiah proved to be disastrous.

Ahaz was succeeded by his son Hezekiah, who was everything his father was not.

> He destroyed the pagan places of worship...and cut down the images of the goddess Asherah...Hezekiah trusted in the Lord, the God of Israel; Judah never had another king like him...So the Lord was with him and he was successful in everything he did. (2 Kings 18:4-7)

It was Hezekiah's wish that only Yahweh would be worshipped throughout Judah, a reversal from this father's aberrations that was certainly supported by Isaiah.

It was during the reign of Hezekiah that Assyria completed its annexation of Israel in 721 BCE, deporting many of its leading citizens into exile. It was only a matter of time before Assyria continued south to assimilate Judah as well. This began in 701 BCE, when the Assyrian emperor Sennacherib conquered several of the cities of northern Judah. Hezekiah attempted to placate Sennacherib with a tribute of gold and silver, but Sennacherib continued his southward advance, planning an attack on Jerusalem. Again, Isaiah entered the picture when Hezekiah requested his advice.

Isaiah told Hezekiah,

> The Lord tells you not to let the Assyrians frighten you with their claims that He cannot save you. The Lord will cause the emperor to hear a rumor that will make him go back to his own country, and the Lord will have him killed there. (Isaiah 19:6-7)

Hezekiah listened to Isaiah and placed his trust in the Lord.

> That night an angel of the Lord went to the Assyrian camp and killed 185,000 soldiers. At dawn the next day there they lay, all dead! Then the Assyrian emperor Sennacherib withdrew and returned to Nineveh [the capital of Assyria]. One day, when he was worshiping in the temple of his god Nisroch, two of his sons, Adrammelech and Sharezer, killed him with their swords and

> then escaped to the land of Ararat. Another of his sons, Esarhaddon, succeeded him as emperor. *(Isaiah 19:35-37)*

Again, trust in the Lord had been rewarded, and Isaiah's advice had been proven invaluable.

Much of the remaining portions of chapters 7-39 can be described as a series of threats and warnings tempered with promises of restoration and reconciliation. For example, Yahweh threatened the destruction of Babylon, Assyria, Philistia and Moab (for various reasons) in chapters fourteen and fifteen. Punishments would be directed against Syria, Israel, Ethiopia and Egypt, as specified in chapters seventeen through nineteen. But other foretellings portrayed something much more positive - a future reunification of God's people:

> *A day is coming when the new king from the royal line of David will be a symbol to the nations...When that day comes, the Lord will...bring back home those of His people who are left is Assyria and Egypt...Pathros, Ethiopia, Elam, Babylonia and Hamath...in the coastlands, and on the islands of the sea. The Lord...is gathering together...the scattered people of Israel and Judah and bringing them back from the four corners of the earth. (Isaiah 11:10-12)*

and...

> *The Lord will once again be merciful to His people Israel and choose them as His own. He will let them live in their own land again, and foreigners will come and live there with them...The Lord will give the people of Israel relief from their pain and suffering and from the hard work they were forced to do. (Isaiah 14:1-3)*

The writings of Isaiah of Jerusalem also feature some of the most beloved and oft-quoted passages in the corpus of the Old Testament. How recognizable are these selections?

> *They will hammer their swords into plows and their spears into pruning knives. Nations will never again go to war, never prepare for battle again. (Isaiah 2:4)*

> *The people who walked in darkness have seen a great light. They lived in a land of shadows, but now light is shining on them. You have given them great joy, Lord; You have made them very happy. (Isaiah 9:2-3)*

> *A child is born to us! A son is given to us! And he will be our ruler. He will be called Wonderful Counselor, Mighty God, Eternal Father, Prince of Peace. His royal power will continue to grow; his kingdom will always be at peace. He will rule as King David's successor, basing his power on right and justice, from now until the end of time. (Isaiah 9:6-7)*

Again, these memorable quotations from Isaiah - at the time they were written - were not viewed by the people of Judah as predictions of a coming Savior, but as indications, perhaps, of more immediate blessings. Interpretation of these words as Messianic predictions would not come until the Babylonian Exile of the next century.

And that leads to one final prediction of Isaiah to Hezekiah. Chapter 38 of Isaiah addresses a serious illness that would lead ultimately to Hezekiah's death.

> *The Lord tells you that you are to put everything in order because you will not recover. Get ready to die. (Isaiah 38:1)*

But it is Hezekiah's behavior in chapter 39 that leads to Isaiah's most fateful and telling prediction. Merodach Baladan, the king of Babylonia, upon hearing of Hezekiah's illness, sent several ambassadors to Jerusalem with gifts for Hezekiah. Hezekiah, perhaps looking to form an alliance with Babylonia against the Assyrians (ignoring Isaiah's warning to place trust in God rather than in political alliances), escorted the ambassadors around his palace, showing off all of his wealth and military equipment - sparing nothing. When Isaiah discovered this, he was crestfallen, revealing:

> *The Lord Almighty says that a time is coming when everything in your palace, everything that your ancestors have stored up to this day, will be carried off to Babylonia. Nothing will be left. Some of your own direct descendants will be*

> *taken away and made eunuchs to serve in the palace of the king of Babylonia. (Isaiah 39:5)*

Yet again, placing trust in the Lord alone and following the dictates of His Covenant will be rewarded, but failing to do these things will result in dire consequences. Isaiah indicates that, while Jerusalem was spared from an attack by Sennacherib's Assyrian forces, it would be at the hands of the Babylonians that punishment for failure to follow the Covenant would be meted.

Upon Hezekiah's death, his son Manasseh ascended to the throne and, unfortunately, his reign was a reversal of the spiritually inspired reign of his father.

> *Manasseh sinned against the Lord. He rebuild the pagan places of worship that his father Hezekiah had destroyed; he built altars for the worship of Baal…and Asherah…Manasseh also worshiped the stars. He built pagan altars in the Temple, the place that the Lord had said was where He should be worshiped… He sacrificed his son as a burnt offering. He practiced divination and magic, and consulted fortune tellers and mediums. (Isaiah 21:2-6)*

Manasseh's rule marked a low point in the history of Judah in much the same way that Ahab's rule was a spiritually bankrupt era for Israel. No information is recorded in Scripture about the death of Isaiah of Jerusalem, but it has traditionally been asserted that he was killed by Manasseh. There is no evidence to support this, but since

> *Manasseh killed so many innocent people that the streets of Jerusalem were flowing with blood… (2 Kings 21:19)*

it isn't a far-fetched conclusion.

DEUTERO-ISAIAH: WORDS OF ENCOURAGEMENT

Chapter 40 in the Book of Isaiah offers a seismic shift in timbre, content and temporal placement. The scene fast-forwards to roughly 150 years in the future, and the audience of chapters 40-55 is a Judean population that has largely been exiled and enslaved in Babylonia by King Nebuchadnezzar, as predicted by Isaiah to Hezekiah. As mentioned earlier, there is a strong difference of opinion between Biblical scholars who maintain that these chapters must have been written by a different, later author or authors (called "Second Isaiah" or "Deutero-Isaiah" due to lack of a more specific identity) and those who maintain that Isaiah of Jerusalem is the sole author of the entire Book, blessed with insights from the Lord that allowed him to offer specific information about distant, future events. In either event, chapters 40-55 are clearly addressed to a later audience with a very different message.

Professor of Old Testament Studies Claude Mariottini of Northern Baptist Seminary, on his personal website www.claudemariottini.com, explained the difference: "The message of Deutero-Isaiah is a message that God has come to redeem His people from their exile...a herald of good news. The people who are now living in the darkness of exile are promised the light of a new day. Deutero-Isaiah proclaims a message of consolation to a hopeless and despairing people. The people have suffered severely for their sins, but that now is in the past."

In the century and a half that elapsed between chapters 39 and 40, the Assyrians, who had obliterated Israel and dominated Judah, were in turn defeated by the ascending Babylonians, who eventually set their own sights on Judah - initially "vassalizing" it, then overrunning it and leveling Jerusalem before ultimately hauling a sizable percentage of the Judean population to a life of slavery in Babylon. This "Babylonian Captivity" or "Exile" extended from 587 to 539 BCE, and more specific details about this very difficult time can be found in the ministries of both Jeremiah and Ezekiel. It was a time when the people of Judah felt abandoned by Yahweh, despite the fact that He had sent them countless warnings that their violations of the Covenant would be punished by desecration of their land, captivity and exile unless they were to return to the spirit of the Covenant.

The opening words of chapter 40 instantly reveal that "the times, they are a-changing:"

> "Comfort, My people," says our God. "Comfort them! Encourage the people of Jerusalem. Tell them they have suffered long enough and their sins are now forgiven. I have punished them in full for all their sins." (Isaiah 40:1-2)

This theme that Judah's expiation for its sinfulness was now coming to its conclusion resounded over and over again in the words of Deutero-Isaiah:

> I will lead My blind people by roads they have never traveled. I will turn their darkness into light and make rough country smooth before them. These are My promises and I will keep them without fail."(Isaiah 42:16)
>
> Israel, the Lord Who created you says, "Do not be afraid - I will save you. I have called you by name - you are Mine." (Isaiah 43:1)
>
> Do not be afraid - I am with you! From the distant east and the farthest west I will bring your people home. I will tell the north to let them go and the south not to hold them back. Let My people return from distant lands, from every part of the world. They are My own people, and I created them to bring Me glory. (Isaiah 43:5-7)

As famous as Deutero-Isaiah is for these words of comfort and consolation, the chapters written by this author hold a special place in Biblical literature for the presence of four "Songs of the Suffering Servant," as they are usually called. These four songs/poems describe the characteristics and experiences of a servant of God, without offering any further clues as to his identity. The first Servant Song:

> The Lord says, "Here is My servant, whom I strengthen - the one I have chosen, with whom I am pleased.
>
> I have filled him with My spirit, and he will bring justice to every nation.
>
> He will not shout or raise his voice or make loud speeches in the streets.
>
> He will not break off a bent reed nor put out a flickering lamp.
>
> He will bring lasting justice to all.
>
> He will not lose hope or courage; he will establish justice on the earth.

Distant lands eagerly wait for his teaching." (Isaiah 42:1-4)

As with the remaining three Servant Songs, the identity of this Servant is the subject of ongoing debate.

For the audience of Deutero-Isaiah, the Servant was most probably thought to represent the nation of Judah as a whole. This may have been consistent with the author's message that Yahweh had forgiven their iniquities and would restore His Chosen People to a position of prominence and honor in a world seeking virtuous leadership. This first Song is delivered from the mouth of God.

The second Servant Song is found in Isaiah 49:1-6:

Listen to me, distant nations, you people who live far away!

Before I was born, the Lord chose me and appointed me to be His servant.

He made my words as sharp as a sword. With His own hand He protected me.

He made me like an arrow, sharp and ready for use.

He said to me, "Israel, you are My servant; because of you, people will praise Me."

I said, "I have worked, but how hopeless it is! I have used up my strength, but have accomplished nothing."

Yet I can trust the Lord to defend my cause; He will reward me for what I do.

Before I was born, the Lord appointed me; He made me His servant to bring back His people, to bring back the scattered people of Israel.

The Lord gives me honor; He is the source of my strength.

The Lord said to me, "I have a greater task for you, My servant. Not only will you restore to greatness the people of Israel who have survived, but I will also make you a light to the nations - so that all the world may be saved."

This second Servant Song is interpreted by some (as was true of the first Song) to suggest that Israel itself is the unnamed Servant. The line "Israel, you are My servant" explicitly proclaims that. Yet, in his 1992 text *The Major Prophets*, Dr. James E. Smith of Florida Christian College (now Johnson University Florida) felt quite differently: "The second Servant poem focuses on the work and success of God's Servant. That the Servant would be an individual with a worldwide mission of redemption is made quite clear." Again, opinions clearly differ, but what is clear is that this second Song, delivered by the Servant, expresses the parameters of his call narrative as well as his acceptance of the ministry entrusted to him.

The third Servant Song follows closely after the second in chapter 50:4-9:

> *The Sovereign Lord has taught me what to say, so that I can strengthen the weary.*
>
> *Every morning He makes me eager to hear what He is going to teach me.*
>
> *The Lord has given me understanding, and I have not rebelled or turned away from Him.*
>
> *I bared my back to those who beat me. I did not stop them when they insulted me, when they pulled out the hairs of my beard and spit in my face.*
>
> *But their insults cannot hurt me because the Sovereign Lord gives me help.*
>
> *I brace myself to endure them. I know that I will not be disgraced, for God is near, and He will prove me innocent.*
>
> *Does anyone dare bring charges against me? Let us go to court together! Let him bring his accusation!*
>
> *The Sovereign Lord Himself defends me - who, then, can prove me guilty?*
>
> *All my accusers will disappear; they will vanish like moth-eaten cloth.*

The third Song, spoken by the Servant himself, expresses confidence that he is prepared and willing to begin his ministry - even to the point of suffering hardships to complete it. It also depicts a Servant who is convinced of the righteousness of his calling and his eventual vindication, if vindication is necessary.

The fourth and final Servant Song - the longest of the four - has been called both the greatest and the best-known of the Songs. It is composed as a dialogue between God and His people, and it is the details expressed in this Song that have led so many Christians to view this Song as a foretelling of the trials and tribulations that Jesus was forced to endure as expiation for the sins of humanity.

> *The Lord says, "My servant will succeed in his task; he will be highly honored.*
>
> *Many people were shocked when they saw him; he was so disfigured that he hardly looked human.*
>
> *But now many nations will marvel at him, and kings will be speechless with amazement.*
>
> *They will see and understand something they had never known."*
>
> *The people reply, "Who would have believed what we now report? Who could have seen the Lord's hand in this?*
>
> *It was the will of the Lord that His servant grow like a plant taking root in dry ground.*
>
> *He had no dignity or beauty to make us take notice of him.*
>
> *There was nothing attractive about him, nothing that would draw us to him.*
>
> *We despised him and rejected him; he endured suffering and pain.*
>
> *No one would even look at him - we ignored him as if he were nothing.*
>
> *But he endured the suffering that should have been ours, the pain that we should have borne.*
>
> *All the while we thought that his suffering was punishment sent by God.*
>
> *But because of our sins he was wounded, beaten because of the evil we did.*
>
> *We are healed by the punishment he suffered, made whole by the blows he received.*

All of us were like sheep that were lost, each of us going his own way.

But the Lord made the punishment fall on him, the punishment all of us deserved.

He was treated harshly, but endured it humbly; he never said a word.

Like a lamb about to be slaughtered, like a sheep about to be sheared, he never said a word.

He was arrested and sentenced and led off to die, and no one cared about his fate.

He was put to death for the sins of our people.

He was placed in a grave with evil men, he was buried with the rich, even though he had never committed a crime or ever told a lie."

The Lord says, "It was My will that he should suffer; his death was a sacrifice to bring forgiveness.

And so he will see his descendants; he will live a long life, and through him My purpose will succeed.

After a life of suffering, he will again have joy; he will know that he did not suffer in vain.

My devoted servant, with whom I am pleased, will bear the punishment of many and for his sake I will forgive them.

And so I will give him a place of honor, a place among great and powerful men.

He willingly gave his life and shared the fate of evil men.

He took the place of many sinners and prayed that they might be forgiven."
(Isaiah 52:13 -53:12)

The final two chapters of Deutero-Isaiah re-affirm the Lord's promise of forgiveness and perpetual love as well as the release of His people from the oppression of their captors.

> *Israel, you are like a young wife, deserted by her husband and deeply distressed.*
>
> *But the Lord calls you back to Him and says: "For one brief moment I left you; with deep love I will take you back. I turned away angry for only a moment, but I will show you My love forever...In the time of Noah I promised never again to flood the earth.*
>
> *Now I promise not to be angry with you again; I will not reprimand or punish you.*
>
> *The mountains and hills may crumble, but My love for you will never end; I will keep forever My promise of peace." So says the Lord Who loves you. (Isaiah 54:6-10)*

And to be specific about the end of captivity:

> *You will leave Babylon with joy; you will be led out of the city in peace.*
>
> *The mountains and hills will burst into singing, and the trees will shout for joy.*
>
> *Cypress trees will grow where now there are briers; myrtle trees will come up in place of thorns.*
>
> *This will be a sign that will last forever, a reminder of what I, the Lord, have done. (Isaiah 55:12-13)*

There is one final note of importance regarding the work of "Deutero-Isaiah" - and this lies at the root of the controversy surrounding the true authorship of chapters 40-55. While many prophets made predictions of one kind or another about future events, these predictive comments were rarely specific or substantive. However, the mention of King Cyrus the Great *by name* in chapters 44 and 45 begs the question: could Isaiah of Jerusalem really have named the king who would release the Judeans from captivity 150 years in advance - when the Judeans hadn't even been exiled yet? It is this specificity that has led many to believe that a different - and much later - author had to have written this section of the Book of Isaiah:

I say to Cyrus, "You are the one who will rule for Me; you will do what I want you to do: you will order that Jerusalem be rebuilt and that the foundations of the Temple be laid."

The Lord has chosen Cyrus to be king.

He has appointed him to conquer nations; He sends him to strip kings of their power; the Lord will open gates of the cities for him.

To Cyrus the Lord says, "I Myself will prepare your way, leveling mountains and hills.

I will break down bronze gates and smash their iron bars.

I will give you treasures from dark, secret places; then you will know that I am the Lord and that the God of Israel has called you by name.

I appoint you to help My servant Israel, the people that I have chosen.

I have given you great honor, although you do not know Me." (Isaiah 44:28 - 45:4)

TRITO-ISAIAH: RIGHTEOUS LIVING AND PROMISES OF GLORY

The Babylonian Captivity of the Judeans ended in 539 BCE when the Persian Empire under Cyrus the Great defeated the Babylonians. While Cyrus was technically the conqueror of the Judeans - both those who were held captive in Babylon as well as those who remained in Judea - the Judeans viewed Cyrus more as a liberator than as a conqueror. Cyrus considered the Judeans to be citizens of the Persian Empire and, as such, they were permitted to remain in Babylon or return to their homeland of Judea. His treatment of them was much more humane than their life under Babylonian rule. Some left Babylon for Judea, while some remained. Chapters 56-66 of Isaiah are believed to have been written between the end of the Captivity (539 BCE) and about 510 BCE. Its author is thought to be a disciple (or disciples) of Deutero-Isaiah.

Given the arbitrary appellation of "Trito-Isaiah" (or "Third Isaiah"), the author wrote specifically to the Judeans who opted to return to their homeland to rebuild. But his words, which offered a glimpse of the future glory that awaited the Chosen People, were predicated - as always - on their conformity to the stipulations of the Covenant. Returning to freedom in Jerusalem from captivity in Babylon guaranteed nothing in the way of added blessings, unless those blessings were earned.

The first four chapters of Trito-Isaiah remind the Judeans of God's expectations and the sinfulness that resulted in their exile and captivity.

> *The Lord says to His people, "Do what is just and right, for soon I will save you. I will bless those who always observe the Sabbath and do not misuse it. I will bless those who do nothing evil." (Isaiah 56:1-2)*

Their penchant for idolatry and the other sinful practices that flow from it are especially condemned:

> *You are no better than sorcerers, adulterers and prostitutes...You worship the fertility gods by having sex under those sacred trees of yours. You offer your children as sacrifices...You take smooth stones and worship them as gods. You pour out wine as offerings to them and bring them grain offerings. Do you think I am pleased with all this? You go to the high mountains to offer sacrifices and have sex. You set up your obscene idols just inside your front doors. You forsake Me; you take off your clothes and climb in your large beds with your lovers, whom you pay to sleep with you. And there you satisfy your lust. You put on your perfumes and ointments and go to worship the god Molech. To find gods to worship, you send messengers far and wide, even to the world of the dead...Who are these gods that make you afraid, so that you tell Me lies and forget Me completely? (Isaiah 57:3-11)*

The people were also reminded that empty, superficial rituals are unacceptable. Religious observance to honor Yahweh must be sincere - and reflect genuine commitment and devotion:

> *The Lord says, "My people...worship Me every day, claiming that they are eager to know My ways and obey My laws. They say they want Me to give*

them just laws and that they take pleasure in worshipping Me." The people ask, "Why should we fast if the Lord never notices? Why should we go without food if He pays no attention?"

The Lord says to them, "The truth is that at the same time you fast, you pursue your own interests and oppress your workers. Your fasting makes you violent, and you quarrel and fight. Do you think this kind of fasting will make Me listen to your prayers?...

The kind of fasting I want is this: Remove the chains of oppression and the yoke of injustice, and let the oppressed go free. Share your food with the hungry and open your homes to the homeless poor. Give clothes to those who have nothing to wear, and do not refuse to help your own relatives. Then My favor will shine on you like the morning sun, and your wounds will be quickly healed. I will always be with you to save you; My presence will protect you on every side. When you pray, I will answer you.

When you call to Me, I will respond." (Isaiah 58:1-8)

Theologian J. Daniel Hays in *The Message of the Prophets* pointed out that the priorities articulated by Yahweh through Trito-Isaiah placed great emphasis on genuine compassion and aid to the *anawim* - the most unfortunate and downtrodden members of Judean society - coupled with acts of authentic piety and moral uprightness rather than empty religious ritual observance.

Trito-Isaiah goes on to paint a picture of the glory that awaits the Judeans if they "straighten up and fly right." The determining factor is the "IF" - future glory is dependent on their willingness and ability to follow God's commands, but the glory does await them:

Arise, Jerusalem, and shine like the sun; the glory of the Lord is shining on you!

Other nations will be covered by darkness, but on you the light of the Lord will shine;

The brightness of His presence will be with you.

> *Nations will be drawn to your light, and kings to the dawning of your new day...Foreigners will rebuild your walls, and their kings will serve you.*
>
> *In My anger I punished you, but now I will show you My favor and mercy... The wood of the pine, the juniper, and the cypress, the finest wood from the forests of Lebanon, will be brought to rebuild you, Jerusalem, to make My Temple beautiful, to make My city glorious.*
>
> *The sons of those who oppressed you will come and bow low to show their respect.*
>
> *All who once despised you will worship at your feet.*
>
> *They will call you "The City of the Lord," [and] "Zion, the City of Israel's Holy God."*
>
> *You will no longer be forsaken and hated, a city deserted and desolate.*
>
> *I will make you great and beautiful, a place of joy forever and ever. (Isaiah 60:1-3,10,13-15)*

In chapter 61, the voice shifts suddenly from that of God to that of the Servant. Isaiah 61:1-3 is often considered to be a fifth "Servant Song," reminiscent of the four previous Songs in Deutero-Isaiah. It was these same words that were used by Jesus to announce His ministry to the people over 500 years later:

> *The Sovereign Lord has filled me with His Spirit.*
>
> *He has chosen me and sent me to bring good news to the poor, To heal the broken-hearted, to announce release to captives and freedom to those in prison.*
>
> *He has sent me to proclaim that the time has come when the Lord will save His people and defeat their enemies.*
>
> *He has sent me to comfort all who mourn...*

The Book of Isaiah is a complex and beautiful piece of literature. Whether it was written by one individual or a series of authors spanning the greater part of a quarter-millennium, it made abundantly clear to God's Chosen People what He expected from them in fidelity and practice. And it specified the consequences of both faithful service and failure to serve. It condemned the Judeans' infidelity before its requisite punishment (the Exile), offered encouragement as the Exile was brought to its conclusion, and re-affirmed God's expectations - as well as the consequences of both renewed dedication on the one hand versus a return to abomination on the other. By its concluding words, not one of God's Chosen People could claim ignorance of God's requirements.

CHAPTER 8: QUESTIONS FOR REVIEW

1. Why has the time period covered by the Book of Isaiah become so controversial?
2. What information to we have about the personal life of Isaiah of Jerusalem - his family, his home, his career, etc.
3. What are the details of Isaiah's "call narrative?"
4. Who were the kings of Judah during the time of Isaiah's prophetic ministry? Did they lead Judah well?
5. What role was played by Isaiah's wife and children in his ministry?
6. What parts of the Book of Isaiah are ascribed to Isaiah of Jerusalem, Deutero-Isaiah and Trito-Isaiah? What are their respective themes and who are their respective audiences?
7. According to Isaiah of Jerusalem, what is God's reaction to the worship rituals of the people of Judah? Why does God feel the way He does?
8. Why does Mary Reed Newland compare the "Song of the Vineyard" with a country music ballad?
9. What political decisions made by King Ahaz eventually hurt the people of Judah?
10. Although King Hezekiah was morally and spiritually upright,

what strategic mistake did he make that eventually hurt the people of Judah?
11. At the time of Deutero-Isaiah's "Songs of the Suffering Servant," who was the Servant thought to be?
12. What verses in each of the four Suffering Servant Songs imply that Deutero-Isaiah may have been making predictions of a coming Messiah - Jesus?
13. What is so unusual about the references that Deutero-Isaiah makes about Cyrus, the King of Persia?
14. List 10 sins in the first four chapters of Trito-Isaiah that the author present to the Judeans as especially abhorrent to God.
15. What is the fifth "Suffering Servant Song?" Where is it found and what does it discuss?

Chapter Nine
MICAH

"Bethlehem Ephrathah...out of you I will bring a ruler for Israel..."

The prophet Micah was a contemporary of Isaiah of Jerusalem, Amos and Hosea. Like Amos, he was born in the southern kingdom of Judea, in a small southwestern town called Moresheth, near the border of Philistia. But unlike Amos and Hosea, who ministered in the northern kingdom of Israel, Micah, like Isaiah, was called to his prophetic ministry in his Judean homeland. It is believed that Micah's ministry extended approximately from 738-698 BCE, during the reign of Kings Jotham, Ahaz and Hezekiah. His words and predictions were primarily addressed to the citizens of Jerusalem, the capital of Judea, and Samaria, the capital of Israel.

Little is known of Micah's background. His passionate condemnation of mistreatment of the poor by the rich has led some Biblical scholars to conclude that he himself grappled with poverty, perhaps as a simple farmworker. If so, he was also someone from a rural background railing against greedy city dwellers. Nothing is known of the call narrative that began his prophetic career, nor is any information available about his death. All that we know of Micah can be found in the seven short chapters of his book, but, in those few pages, Micah made his presence felt.

SINS OF THE BIG CITY?

The first three chapters of the Book of Micah are laced with denunciations and threats.

> *The people of Israel have sinned and rebelled against God. Who is to blame for Israel's rebellion? Samaria, the capital city itself! Who is guilty of idolatry in Judea? Jerusalem itself! So the Lord says, "I will make Samaria a pile of ruins in the open country, a place for planting grapevines. I will pour the rubble of the city down into the valley, and will lay bare the city's foundations"...Then Micah said, "...Samaria's wounds cannot be healed, and Judah is about to suffer in the same way; destruction has reached the gates of Jerusalem itself..."*
> (Micah 1:5-6,8-9)

Micah was the first prophet to predict the unthinkable - that Jerusalem, the city of David, could be destroyed. Judeans believed that God lived in Jerusalem and would protect it - no matter what - so any prediction of its downfall was not only laughable, but traitorous. Micah even discussed this misconception:

> The people preach at me and say, "Don't preach at us...God is not going to disgrace us...Has the Lord lost His patience? Would he really do such things?" (Micah 2:6-7)

But his response was uncompromising.

> The Lord replies, "You attack My people like enemies. Men return from battle, thinking they are safe at home, but there you are, waiting to steal the coats off their backs. You drive the women...out of the homes they love, and you have robbed their children of My blessings forever. Get up and go; there is no safety here anymore, Your sins have doomed this place to destruction." (Micah 2:8-10)

Micah went on to denounce the leaders who "hate what is good and ...love what is evil," taking advantage of those they were expected to protect and defend. His description of the way they took advantage of the less fortunate was quite graphic:

> You skin my people alive and tear the flesh off their bones. You eat my people up. You strip off their skin, break their bones, and chop them up like meat for the pot. (Micah 3:2-3)

Micah was not one to mince words (no pun intended).

The exploitation of the poor was not the sole province of the political leaders. Entrepreneurs and shopkeepers were equally guilty.

> The Lord... calls to the city, "Listen, you people who assemble in the city. In the houses of evil men are treasures which they got dishonestly. They use false measures, a thing that I hate. How can I forgive men who use false scales and weights? You rich men exploit the poor, and all of you are liars. So I have

> *already begun your ruin and destruction because of your sins." (Micah 6:9-13)*

Likewise, he condemned prophets who deliberately misled the people, basing their predictions solely on payments received. He contrasted their "ministries" with his own.

> *But as for me, the Lord fills me with His Spirit and power, and gives me a sense of justice and the courage to tell the people...what their sins are. Listen to me, you rulers of Israel...You are building God's city, Jerusalem, on a foundation of murder and injustice. The city's rulers govern for bribes, the priests interpret the law for pay, the prophets give their revelations for money - and they all claim that the Lord is with them...And so, because of you, Zion will be plowed like a field, Jerusalem will become a pile of ruins, and the Temple hill will become a forest. (Micah 3:8-12)*

Like Isaiah of Jerusalem, his contemporary, Micah also alluded to a future exile as punishment for the sins of the people - and he specified Babylon as the site of this exile.

> *Twist and groan, people of Jerusalem, like a woman giving birth, for now you will have to leave the city and live in the open country. You will have to go to Babylon, but there the Lord will save you from your enemies. (Micah 4:10)*

Micah's ministry was not completely saturated with denouncements, accusations and threats. He also envisioned a future characterized by universal peace, centered around dedication to Yahweh:

> *In days to come the mountain where the Temple stands will be the highest one of all, towering above all the hills.*
>
> *Many nations will come streaming to it, and their people will say, "Let us go up the hill of the Lord, to the Temple of Israel's God.*
>
> *He will teach us what He wants us to do; we will walk in the paths He has chosen.*

For the Lord's teaching comes from Jerusalem; from Zion He speaks to His people."

He will settle disputes among the nations, among the great powers near and far.

They will hammer their swords into plows and their spears into pruning knives.

Nations will never again go to war, never prepare for battle again.

Everyone will live in peace among his own vineyards and fig trees, and no one will make him afraid.

The Lord Almighty has promised this. (Micah 4:1-4)

How would this time of universal peace be brought to fruition? Micah's answer to this constitutes his most famous prediction:

The Lord says, "Bethlehem Ephrathah, you are one of the smallest towns in Judea, but out of you I will bring a ruler for Israel, whose family line goes back to ancient times."...When he comes, he will rule his people with the strength that comes from the Lord and with the majesty of the Lord God Himself. His people will live in safety because people all over the earth will acknowledge his greatness, and he will bring peace. (Micah 5:2-4)

Christians, of course, look to this prediction of Micah and attribute it to the birth of Jesus in Bethlehem, as chronicled in the Gospels of Matthew and Luke.

Of all the prophets of the Old Testament who attempted to explain and summarize how God expected His people to show their love and fidelity, perhaps no one has expressed it more eloquently and succinctly than Micah: *...to do what is right, to show constant love, and to live in humble fellowship with our God. (Micah 6:8)*

CHAPTER 9: QUESTIONS FOR REVIEW

1. Where and when did Micah exercise his prophetic ministry? What kings reigned at this time?
2. What is known of Micah's background and personal life? What is presumed about him?
3. Micah denounced many different people for the sins and crimes of his era, Who were his targets?
4. Why did Micah condemn some of the priests and prophets of his time?
5. What troubling predictions did Micah make about the city of Jerusalem and the country of Babylon?
6. What did Micah have to say about a small, backwater village known as Bethlehem?
7. What quotation of Micah from Chapter 6 of his book best summarized God's expectation for his Chosen People?

Chapter Ten
EZEKIEL

"Mortal man...I am sending you to the people of Israel"

*A*merican musician and composer Oscar Levant once said, "There's a fine line between genius and insanity. I have erased this line." Certainly, many psychologists and psychiatrists have similarly researched the relationship between genius and insanity as well. While we may never know if the prophet Ezekiel possessed the requisite IQ to be labeled a genius, we do know that Ezekiel's bizarre symbolic gestures and vivid, disturbing visions led many of his contemporaries to believe that he was, indeed, insane - or in some other way mentally disturbed. We have come to the subsequent conclusion that this "lay diagnosis" is untrue, but the fact that it is a topic of discussion demonstrates that this man was clearly a very interesting - if perhaps deeply troubled - individual.

POLITICAL TURBULENCE

To appreciate the ministry and message of Ezekiel, who wore "two hats" as both priest and prophet, it is necessary to understand the political climate in which he lived. The death of the evil, idolatrous King Manasseh in 643 BCE and the assassination of his son Amon in 641 BCE led to the ascendancy of his 8-year-old son, King Josiah. Josiah reigned until he was killed in battle by the Egyptians in 609 BCE, but during his reign, he initiated a series of spiritual reforms and tried to return Judah from its idolatrous ways to the worship of Yahweh alone. He is often considered the last "good king" of Judah.

Josiah's death brought his son Jehoahaz to the throne, but the Egyptian victory over Judah led the Egyptian King Neco II to sack Judah of its treasures and place Jehoahaz' brother Jehoiakim on the throne as a vassal king. When the powerful Babylonian army under crown prince Nebuchadnezzar defeated the Egyptians in 605 BCE, Jehoiakim switched allegiance to Babylon, pledging himself as a vassal to Nebuchadnezzar, who became king of Babylon upon the death of his father Nabopolassar. Nebuchadnezzar was as ruthless as he was strategic. In 606 BCE, he took several royal hostages from Jerusalem to "encourage" Jehoiakim to remain a faithful vassal. Included among these hostages was Daniel, who would go on to establish himself as a powerful prophet and political administrator in years to come. (He will be discussed more fully in Chapter 12)

In 601 BCE, the Babylonian army engaged the Egyptians in battle, but were forced to retreat. This prompted Jehoiakim again to switch allegiances and support Egypt. Although Nebuchadnezzar had lost this battle, his power was still formidable, and he elected to teach a lesson to Jehoiakim (and any other vassals considering disloyalty to him) by sacking Jerusalem. The year was 597 BCE. Jehoiakim was killed in the ensuing battle, supplanted as king by his young son Jehoiachin (also called Jeconiah). Jehoiachin surrendered to Nebuchadnezzar rather than see his capital city destroyed, and after a reign of only three months, he was deported to Babylon, along with other members of the royal family and assorted officials and craftsmen. Included among these deportees was the priest Ezekiel. Nebuchadnezzar plundered the treasures of Jerusalem and installed Jehoiachin's uncle Mattaniah (whose name he changed to Zedekiah) as the new vassal king. It was during Ezekiel's deportation to Babylon that his prophetic ministry began, circa 593 BCE. His messages were delivered primarily to the other Judeans held captive in Babylon. Meanwhile, Jeremiah was called by God to a prophetic ministry to those left behind in Judea. His ministry will be discussed more fully in the next chapter.

EZEKIEL'S CALL NARRATIVE

According to Ezekiel himself, his call narrative began in a quite dramatic fashion during his fifth year in captivity in Babylon.

> *I, Ezekiel, the priest, son of Buzi, was living with the Jewish exiles by the Chebar River in Babylonia. The sky opened and I saw a vision of God. It was the fifth year since King Jehoiachin had been taken into exile...I heard the Lord speak to me, and I felt His power. (Ezekiel 1:1-3)*

In vivid detail, the first three chapters of the Book of Ezekiel outlined this mystical, spiritual experience. Ezekiel described a windstorm with lightning, out of which emerged four creatures, each of whom had four faces, four wings and four hands. Their feet were hoofed and their skins were like polished bronze, and each of their four faces was different: a human face, a lion's face, an eagle's face and the face of an ox. With their spread wings touching one another, they moved as a unit. The creatures were joined by rotating wheels, looking something like gyroscopes, whose rims were filled with eyes. There was a crystal dome above the heads of the four creatures, and on the dome, on a sapphire throne, sat a figure who resembled a man, shining like bronze. He radiated a bright light that contained all the colors of the rainbow - showing that this was the presence of the Lord.

Ezekiel said he fell on his face, but was raised up by God, Who said:

> *Mortal man, I am sending you to the people of Israel. They have rebelled and turned against Me and are still rebels, just as their ancestors were. They are stubborn and do not respect Me, and I am sending you to tell them what I, the Sovereign Lord, am saying to them. Whether those rebels listen to you or not, they will know that a prophet has been among them. (Ezekiel 2:3-5)*

Ezekiel was then asked to eat a scroll that was handed to him, and

> *"...it tasted as sweet as honey." (Ezekiel 3:3)*

Upon his return to the exiles, Ezekiel said it took him seven days to recover from this intense revelation.

While the ministry of Ezekiel is duly recorded in the Book named after him, the hallmark of Ezekiel's ministry lay less in his spoken word and more in his symbolic gestures and dramatic visions. It was largely as a result of these tools that Ezekiel used to convey God's messages and warnings to the people that Ezekiel was often thought to be mentally unbalanced. Unlike many of the other Prophetic Books of the Old Testament, the visions and symbolic actions of Ezekiel are, for the most part, recorded in chronological order.

From the outset of his ministry, Ezekiel found himself placed under very strict limitations by God.

The Lord said to me, "Go home and shut yourself up in the house...you will not be able to go out in public. I will paralyze your tongue so that you won't be able to warn these rebellious people. Then, when I speak to you again and give you back the power of speech, you will tell them what I, the Sovereign Lord, am saying." (Ezekiel 3:24-27)

These restrictions, of course, were not absolute. There were many instances of Ezekiel verbally delivering God's messages to the people. But these restrictions do seem to contradict Ezekiel's prophetic calling. It has been suggested that God required Ezekiel to remain in his home to protect himself from incarceration by those who didn't want to hear his pronouncements. It has also been posited that the imposition of silence was on Ezekiel as an individual and not as a prophet. His ability to speak was intact any time God gave him a message to pass along to the people. Still, Ezekiel's ministry is remembered primarily for his dramatic, symbolic actions and vivid visions.

SYMBOLIC ACTIONS

Ezekiel's first symbolic act, as mandated by God, involved forming a scale model of Jerusalem out of a brick, an iron pan and sticks and stones to represent the upcoming siege of Jerusalem by Babylon. Ezekiel was required to lay on his left side for 390 days (representing the temporal punishment of Israel), and then on his right side for 40 days (representing the temporal punishment of Judah), to demonstrate how Jerusalem will be attacked from all sides - and how God will observe this but do nothing to help. His food and water was likewise limited during the time he lay there - just 2 cups of water and 8 ounces of bread - to represent the food shortages and rationing that the citizens of Jerusalem would have to endure as a result of the siege. Throughout this time, Ezekiel was also required to

shake your fist at the city and prophesy against it. (Ezekiel 4:7)

Shortly thereafter, the Lord instructed Ezekiel to

> take a sharp sword and use it to shave off your beard and all your hair...and divide it into three parts. Burn up a third of it...Take another third and chop it up...Scatter the remaining third to the winds. Keep back a few hairs and keep them in the hem of your clothes... (Ezekiel 5:1-4)

The shaven hair was meant to represent the citizens of Jerusalem. In the upcoming siege, as the Lord explained to Ezekiel:

> A third of your people will die from sickness and hunger in the city; a third will be cut down by swords outside the city; and I will scatter the last third to the winds and pursue them with a sword. (Ezekiel 5:11-12)

The remaining hairs that were hidden away represented those who would eventually return (called the *remnant*) and begin the process of reconstruction.

The Lord's instructions to Ezekiel to present symbolic actions were far from over. Next, the Lord said:

> Now, mortal man, pack a bundle just as a refugee would and start out before nightfall. Let everyone see you leaving and going to another place...While it is still daylight, pack your bundle for exile, so that they can see you, and then let them watch you leave in the evening as if you were going into exile. While they are watching, break a hole through the wall of your house and take your pack out through it. Let them watch you putting your pack on your shoulder and going out into the dark with your eyes covered, so that you can't see where you are going. What you do will be a warning to the Israelites. (Ezekiel 12:3-6)

Ezekiel did as the Lord commanded, and his strange behavior piqued the interest of the onlookers. The Lord then instructed Ezekiel to answer their questions and explain His message:

> ...Tell them what I, the Sovereign Lord, am saying to them. This message is for the prince ruling in Jerusalem and for all the people who live there. Tell them that what you have done is a sign of what will happen to them - they will be refugees and captives. The prince who is ruling them will shoulder his pack in the dark and escape through a hole that they dig for him in the wall. He will

> cover his eyes and not see where he is going. But I will spread out My net and trap him in it. Then I will take him to the city of Babylon, where he will die without having seen it. (Ezekiel 12:10-13)

At the time King Jehoiachin and the members of his court (including Ezekiel) were banished to Babylon by Nebuchadnezzar in 597 BCE and Jehoiachin's uncle Mattaniah was installed as vassal King Zedekiah, neither the Judean exiles sent to Babylon nor the Judeans who remained in their homeland thought that further punishments would be visited upon Judah - much less that Jerusalem would ultimately be destroyed and its citizens exiled ten years later. If anything, the prevailing thought was that God Himself lived in Jerusalem, and the city was inviolable. Therefore, symbolic actions such as this one - designed to offer a glimpse of even more disastrous punishments to be levied against Judah in the future - were shocking to the people. In the case above, Ezekiel's prediction unfolded exactly as stated. King Zedekiah was indeed captured by the Babylonians while attempting to escape through a hole in the wall and brought to Babylon, where he was blinded as he encountered Nebuchadnezzar at the entry to the city. And many of the citizens of Jerusalem either fled or were held in captivity by the Babylonians.

The Lord was not yet finished with Ezekiel, whose tasks were perhaps getting more and more difficult to complete. In Ezekiel's own words:

> The Lord spoke to me. "Mortal man...with one blow I am going to take away the person you love most. You are not to complain or cry or shed any tears. Don't let your sobbing be heard. Do not go bareheaded or barefoot as a sign of mourning.
>
> Don't cover your face or eat the food that mourners eat." Early in the day I was talking with the people. That evening my wife died, and the next day I did as I had been told. The people asked me, "Why are you acting like this?" (Ezekiel 24:15-19)

Ezekiel explained to the exiles in Babylon that the members of their families who had been left behind in Jerusalem would be killed, and that the Temple would be desecrated. They would be left in the same position, mourning their dead without the usual trappings of grief and consolation. These were the consequences of ongoing sinfulness and rejection of the Lord.

While each of Ezekiel's gestures heretofore served as a harbinger of doom and despair, his final physical gesture served as a symbol of hope and reconciliation:

> *The Lord spoke to me again. "Mortal man...take a wooden stick and write on it the words 'The Kingdom of Judah.' Then take another stick and write on it the words 'The Kingdom of Israel.' Then hold the two sticks end to end in your hand so they look like one stick. When your people ask you to tell them what this means, tell them that I, the Sovereign Lord, am going to take the stick representing Israel and put it with the one that represents Judah. Out of the two I will make one stick and hold it in My hand...Tell them that I...am going to take all My people out of the nations where they have gone, gather them together, and bring them back to their own land. I will unite them into one nation...They will by My people and I will be their God." (Ezekiel 37:16-23)*

VISIONS

Interspersed among the symbolic actions employed by Ezekiel were several vivid and dramatic visions whose details Ezekiel shared with the Judean exiles. His first vision - his call narrative - was replete with powerful images and symbols that overpowered him emotionally as well as spiritually. And some of these same images also appeared in subsequent visions as well. Ezekiel's second vision occurred a year after his prophetic call in the sixth year of his captivity in Babylon.

Ezekiel described how a powerful vision overcame him while sitting in his house with other leaders of the Judeans in exile.

> *Suddenly the power of the Sovereign Lord came on me. I looked up and saw a vision of a fiery human form...He reached out...grabbed me by the hair...lifted me high...and took me to Jerusalem...to the inner entrance of the north gate of the Temple... (Ezekiel 8:2-3)*

He went on to list a series of atrocities that the people of Jerusalem were committing in and around the Temple precincts: placing idols near the altar, incensing graven images within the Temple itself, weeping over the death of the god Tammuz (a Mesopotamian fertility god), and bowing in worship to the rising sun. As the vision unfolded, God voiced His anger at this blatant idolatry.

> The Lord said to me, "Mortal man, do you see that? These people of Judah are not satisfied with merely doing all the disgusting things you have seen here and with spreading violence throughout the country. No, they must come and do them right here in the Temple and make Me even more angry. Look how they insult Me in the most offensive way possible! They will feel all the force of My anger. I will not spare them or show them any mercy." (Ezekiel 8:17-18)

Ezekiel's vision concluded in a terrifying manner, as God sent six executioners to kill all of the inhabitants of Jerusalem who had been unfaithful to Him, sparing only those who rejected the idolatrous ways of their fellow Judeans. When the slaughter was completed, Ezekiel then saw God - in all His glory and surrounded by the same heavenly host of angels from his first vision - rise above Jerusalem and depart the city. God was abandoning His people as a result of their unfaithful abandonment of Him. The same city that all Judeans believed to be the inviolable home of God had now been vacated by the God they had forsaken.

The next vision of Ezekiel goes hand in hand with his joining together of two sticks to represent the reunification of Israel and Judah. Both this gesture and the concomitant vision connected with it are meant to inspire the people that God's punishment of them will end, and ultimately lead to forgiveness and reconciliation. This vision is, perhaps, the vision for which Ezekiel is most well-known. It is called the vision of "the valley of dry bones."

> I felt the powerful presence of the Lord, and His Spirit...set me down in a valley where the ground was covered with bones. He led me all around the valley and I could see that there were very many bones and that they were very dry. He said to me, "Mortal man, can these bones come back to life?" I replied,

"Sovereign Lord, only You can answer that!" He said, "Prophesy to the bones. Tell these dry bones...that I, the Sovereign Lord, am saying to them: I am going to put breath into you and bring you back to life. I will give you sinews and muscles, and cover you with skin...Then you will know that I am the Lord."

So I prophesied as I had been told. While I was speaking, I heard a rattling noise, and the bones began to join together. While I watched, the bones were covered with sinews and muscles, and then with skin. But there was no breath in the bodies.

God said to me, "Prophesy to the wind. Tell the wind that the Sovereign Lord commands it to come from every direction, to breathe into these dead bodies, and to bring them back to life." So I prophesied as I had been told. Breath entered the bodies, and they came to life and stood up. There were enough of them to form an army.

God said to me, "Mortal man, the people of Israel are like these bones. They say that they are dried up, without any hope and with no future. So...tell them that I, the Sovereign Lord, am going to open their graves. I am going to take them out and bring them back to the land of Israel...Then they will know that I am the Lord. I have promised that I would do this - and I will. I, the Lord, have spoken." (Ezekiel 37:1-14)

Ezekiel's final vision came much later - 25 years after King Jehoiachin and his retinue had been exiled to Babylon and fourteen years after Jerusalem had been decimated, as Ezekiel had earlier predicted. This final vision concludes the remaining nine chapters of the Book of Ezekiel and describes in great detail the floor plan of a new Temple to replace the one destroyed by the Babylonians after Yahweh had forsaken it and vacated Jerusalem. Chapter by chapter, the specifications of the new Temple (sometimes referred to as the "Third Temple") are outlined - the four gates, inner and outer courtyards, the central building and nearby buildings, the doors and the altar. Additionally, the vision proscribes rules of admittance into the Temple precincts, the responsibilities of the priests and the administration of rituals and festivals. It specifies the amount and location of the land that was to be allocated to the priests and to the king. But perhaps the most important revelation that emanated from this vision is its pronouncement that Yahweh will return to reside in His new Temple:

> ...I saw coming from the east the dazzling light of the presence of the God of Israel. God's voice sounded like the roar of the sea, and the earth shone with the dazzling light...Then I threw myself face downward on the ground. The dazzling light passed through the east gate and went into the Temple. The Lord's Spirit lifted me up and took me into the inner courtyard where I saw that the Temple was filled with the glory of the Lord...I heard the Lord speak to me out of the Temple: "Mortal man, here is My throne. I will live here among the people of Israel and rule them forever." (Ezekiel 43:2-7)

It was also the Lord's desire that the people of Jerusalem be made aware of the specifications of the new Temple to enable them to construct and plan it properly.

> And the Lord continued, "Mortal man, tell the people of Israel about the Temple, and let them study its plan...explain...its design, its entrances and exits, its shape, the arrangement of everything, and all its rules and regulations. Write all this down for them so that they can see how everything is arranged and can carry out all the rules." (Ezekiel 43:10-11)

The closing line of this revelation (and the last line in the Book of Ezekiel) is perhaps the most jubilant one of all, signaling that the cycle of sinfulness, punishment and reconciliation has come to its final conclusion:

> The name of the city from now on will be "The-Lord-Is-Here." (Ezekiel 48:35)

PARABLES

One final portion of Ezekiel's ministry that is often overlooked is his use of parables to teach the exiles in Babylon. This is probably because both his visions and symbolic gestures are so dramatic that they overshadow the rest of his ministry. His parables are reminiscent of the parables used by Jesus six hundred years later to similarly teach moral lessons to His disciples. Each parable is brought to fruition through a revelation to Ezekiel from the Lord.

Ezekiel's first parable flowed from a series of questions asked of him by God, and its message was yet another dire warning of future punishment.

> "Mortal man...how does a vine compare with a tree? What good is a branch of a grapevine compared with the trees of the forest? Can you use it to make anything?...It is only good for building a fire. And when the ends are burned up and the middle is charred, can you make anything out of it? It was useless even before it was burned. Now that the fire has burned it and charred it, it is even more useless." Now this is what the Sovereign Lord is saying: "Just as a vine is taken from the forest and burned, so I will take the people who live in Jerusalem and will punish them. They have escaped one fire, but now fire will burn them up. When I punish them, you will know that I am the Lord." (Ezekiel 15:1-8)

The second parable used by Ezekiel compares the infidelity of the people of Jerusalem to the behavior of an ungrateful prostitute and speaks very harshly of the consequences of unfaithfulness. This parable is reminiscent of the symbolism used in the marriage of Hosea and Gomer to depict the pain caused by the infidelity of one spouse toward another.

> The Lord spoke to me again. "Mortal man...tell Jerusalem what the Sovereign Lord is saying to her: When you were born...no one took pity on you...no one loved you. You were thrown out in an open field. Then I passed by and saw you...covered with blood, but I wouldn't let you die. I made you grow like a healthy plant. You grew strong and tall and became a young woman...
>
> I saw that the time had come for you to fall in love...I made a marriage covenant with you, and you became Mine...I dressed you in embroidered gowns and gave you shoes of the best leather, a linen headband and a silk cloak. I put jewels on you - bracelets and necklaces...You ate bread made from the best flour, and had honey and olive oil to eat. Your beauty was dazzling, and you became a queen...

> But you took advantage of your beauty and fame to sleep with everyone who came along...just like a prostitute you gave yourself to everyone. You took the silver and gold jewelry that I had given you, used it to make male images, and committed adultery with them. You took the embroidered clothes I gave you and put them on the images, and you offered to the images the olive oil and incense I had given to you. I gave you food - the best flour, olive oil, and honey - but you offered it as a sacrifice to win the favor of idols...Then you took the sons and daughters you had borne Me and offered them as sacrifices to idols...During your disgusting life as a prostitute you never once remembered your childhood - when you were naked, squirming in your own blood."
>
> The Sovereign Lord said, "You are doomed! Doomed!...Now I will raise My hand to punish you and to take away your share of My blessing." (Ezekiel 16:2-23,27)

Ezekiel's third parable was likewise dictated to him by God, and also addressed the theme of unfaithfulness and its consequences.

> The Lord spoke to me. "Mortal man...tell the Israelites a parable to let them know what I, the Sovereign Lord, am saying to them: There was a giant eagle with beautiful feathers and huge wings, spread wide. He flew to the Lebanon Mountains and broke off the top of a cedar tree, which he carried to a land of commerce and placed in a city of merchants. Then he took a young plant from the land of Israel and planted it in a fertile field, where there was always water to make it grow. The plant sprouted and became a low, wide-spreading grapevine.
>
> The branches grew upward toward the eagle, and the roots grew deep. The vine was covered with branches and leaves.
>
> There was another giant eagle with huge wings and thick plumage. And now the vine sent its roots toward him and turned its leaves towards him, in the hope that he would give it more water than there was in the garden where it was growing. But the vine had already been planted in a fertile, well-watered field so that it could grow leaves and bear grapes and be a magnificent vine.

So I, the Sovereign Lord, ask: Will this vine live and grow? Won't the first eagle pull it up by its roots, pull off the grapes, and break off the branches and let them wither?"

The Lord said to me, "Ask these rebels if they know what the parable means.

Tell them that the king of Babylonia came to Jerusalem and took the king and his officials back with him to Babylonia. He took one of the king's family, made a treaty with him, and made him swear to be loyal. He took important men as hostages to keep the nation from rising again and to make sure that the treaty would be kept.

But the king of Judah rebelled and sent agents to Egypt to get horses and a large army. Will he succeed? Can he get away with that? He cannot break the treaty and go unpunished.

As surely as I am the living God...this king will die in Babylonia because he broke his oath and the treaty he had made with the king of Babylonia...I will punish him for breaking the treaty which he swore in My name to keep...I will take him to Babylonia and punish him there, because he was unfaithful to Me. His best soldiers will be killed in battle, and the survivors will be scattered in every direction.

Then you will know that I, the Lord, have spoken." (Ezekiel 17:1-19)

John F. Walvoord and Roy B. Zuck of the Dallas Theological Seminary explained the symbolism of this parable in their 1984 text *The Bible Knowledge Commentary: Major Prophets*: "The first...eagle symbolized Nebuchadnezzar, and Lebanon stood for Jerusalem...The eagle 'clipped the top of a cedar tree and replanted the bough in a city known for trade.' This referred to Nebuchadnezzar's attack on Jerusalem in 597 BCE when he...deposed King Jehoiachin...and replanted the 'shoot' in Babylon. The 'eagle,' Nebuchadnezzar, was not totally heartless. He took a (young plant) and planted it and it 'sprouted and became a low wide-spreading vine.' Nebuchadnezzar weakened Jerusalem, but he did not destroy it...Instead he set up Zedekiah as a vassal king...Zedekiah, a member of the royal family, by a treaty was put under oath. Though Judah was brought low...she could survive if she kept the treaty...The new 'eagle' was Egypt, which influenced Zedekiah to rebel against Babylon. Judah's king violated his oath of allegiance to Babylon and joined forces with Egypt...The results for the vine would be disastrous. Because Zedekiah violated his oath...Nebuchadnezzar would not spare the city...In breaking his oath to Nebuchadnezzar, Zedekiah was also opposing God...God would see that Zedekiah was caught by Nebuchadnezzar...and brought to Babylon with his troops and killed by the sword."

Walvoord and Zuck also pointed out that this prophetic parable was presented by Ezekiel either in 591 or 592 BCE - three years before Zedekiah's revolt against Nebuchadnezzar in 588 BCE.

Ezekiel was a prophet whose ministry, message and lifestyle were different from all the other prophets. The combination of his disturbing visions, dramatic symbolic actions and accusative parables - along with the restrictions placed on him by God (i.e. not to leave his home or to speak unless instructed to do so by God, not to grieve over the death of his wife, to lie prone with minimum food and water for long periods of time, etc.) was absolutely unique. Even though his behaviors could be interpreted as predictive messages from God, he was nevertheless thought by many people to be mentally or psychologically damaged. Neither was true - but he was clearly emotionally overcome by the tragedies he knew were awaiting his people in the days to come. As was true of many of the prophets called to their ministry by God, Ezekiel's life, though clearly blessed by God, was filled with sorrow and despair as much as it heralded future restitution.

CHAPTER 10: QUESTIONS FOR REVIEW

1. What were the circumstances that led Ezekiel to conduct his prophetic ministry in Babylon rather than in Judea?
2. What was so extraordinary about Ezekiel's call narrative?
3. Under what restrictions did God place Ezekiel after calling him to prophethood?
4. What was the symbolic significance of the scale model of Jerusalem built by Ezekiel and the way he behaved when near it?
5. What possessed Ezekiel to shave his beard - and why did he treat the shaved hairs the way he did?
6. What prediction did Ezekiel make about the fate of King Zedekiah of Judea?
7. Why was Ezekiel instructed not to mourn for his wife when she passed away?
8. What was so troubling about Ezekiel's second vision during his sixth year in captivity in Babylon?
9. What is the symbolic significance of Ezekiel's vision of the "valley of dried bones?" was this vision meant to signal impending doom or hope?
10. What is so important about the topic and the message of the

flast vision of Ezekiel that spans the final nine chapters of his book?
11. Ezekiel toward the Judean captives in Babylon by using parables. What was the message and the symbolism he used in his parable of the ungrateful prostitute?
12. What did the two eagles and the vine represent in Ezekiel's third parable?
13. Is it appropriate to characterize Ezekiel as mentally unbalanced? Explain and justify your conclusion.

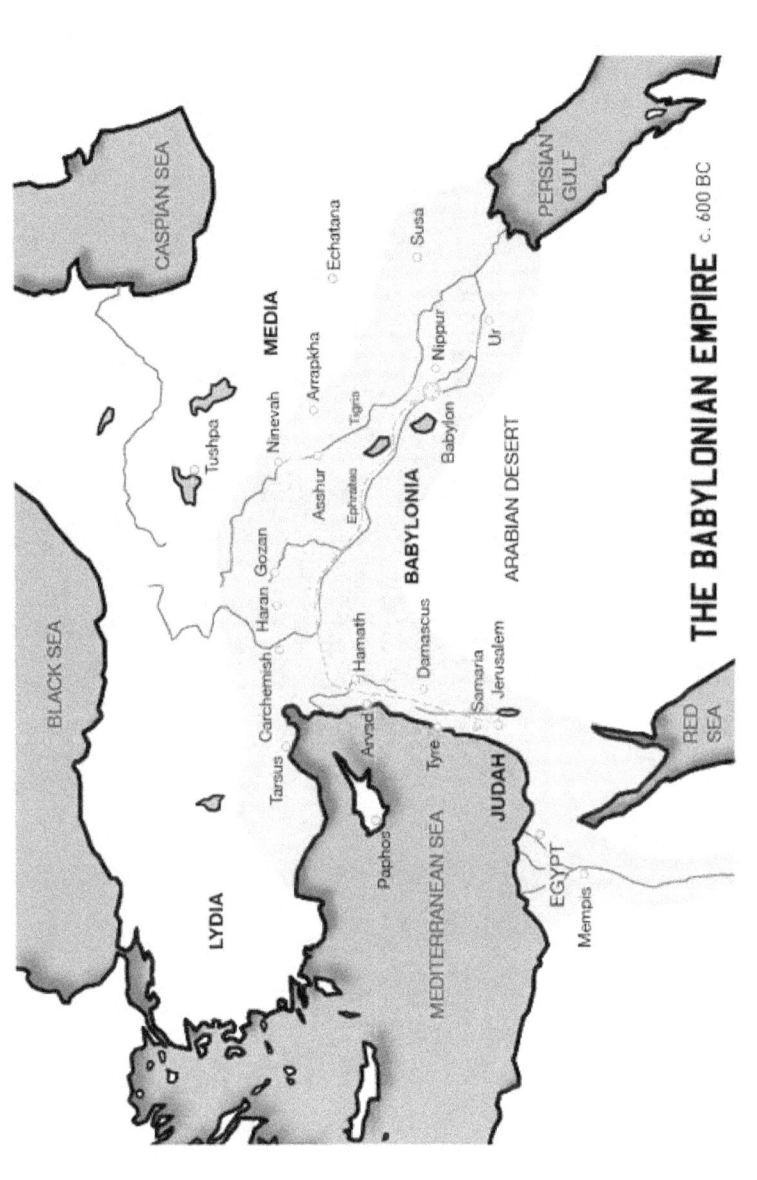

Chapter Eleven
JEREMIAH

"I will put My law within them and write it on their hearts"

Unlike many of his predecessors, whose idolatry and insensitivity to the poor and disenfranchised displeased the Lord greatly, King Josiah of Judah was a spiritual leader whose priority was to return the people of Judah to the proper worship of Yahweh alone. Ascending to the monarchy at the age of eight after the assassination of his father, King Amon, Josiah reigned for thirty-two years, from 641-609 BCE. It was during his reign that he authorized renovations of the Temple in Jerusalem. While these renovations were underway, workers discovered a long-forgotten scroll - "the Book of the Law" - which is thought to have been related to the Old Testament Book of Deuteronomy. Its discovery was instrumental in spearheading the spiritual reforms that highlighted the reign of Josiah.

It was while Josiah was king that Jeremiah was born in the town of Anathoth, about three miles northeast of Jerusalem in Judah. His father Hilkiah was a priest who served the Temple in Jerusalem, and Jeremiah, as a Levite, was expected to follow his father into the priesthood. Jeremiah was born circa 650 BCE and began his prophetic ministry in 627 BCE. His ministry extended through the reigns of Kings Josiah, Jehoahaz, Jehoiakim, Jehoiachin (also known as Jeconiah) and Zedekiah (also known as Mattaniah). Jeremiah lived in incredibly turbulent political times (as outlined at the beginning of the previous chapter on Ezekiel), and it was this political cauldron that served as a backdrop for most of his pronouncements and predictions. The historical details of the times in which Jeremiah lived are outlined in 2 Kings 22-25 and 2 Chronicles 34-36. While Jeremiah was clearly the most dynamic and dominant prophet in Judah, his ministry ran concurrently with the ministries of Habakkuk and Zephaniah in Judah and Ezekiel and Daniel in Babylon.

JEREMIAH'S CALL NARRATIVE

The call narrative of Jeremiah opens the Book named after him. In a vision or dream, Jeremiah first encountered God, Who informed him:

I chose you before I gave you life, and before you were born I selected you to be a prophet to the nations. (Jeremiah 1:5)

When Jeremiah responded that he was too young for such an assignment, the Lord answered:

Do not say that you are too young, but go to the people I send you to, and tell them everything I command you to say. Do not be afraid of them, for I will be with you to protect you. I, the Lord, have spoken! (Jeremiah 1:7-8)

At the time of this revelation, Jeremiah was about 23 years old - young perhaps, but not a child. Rev. David Barton of the Anglican Diocese of Oxford has called Jeremiah "the reluctant prophet" who "does not seem to be made of the stern stuff prophets are supposed to be made of...Sensitive, with an exceptional capacity for affection, he was given a mission 'to pluck up and to break down, to destroy and to overthrow' among the people he loved. This was a path of pain from which, though he might grumble, Jeremiah never flinched." But it was a very difficult ministry for him to undertake.

God presented two visions to Jeremiah at the outset of his ministry. The first was that of an almond tree, which was the Lord's way of letting Jeremiah know that He would be watching to make sure that Jeremiah fulfilled his mission. (In Hebrew, the words for "almond" and "watching" sound very similar, hence the image of the almond tree). The second vision was that of a pot of boiling water, about to tip over southward. This represented the upcoming invasion of the Babylonians from the north to punish the people of Judah in the south for their infidelity.

The Lord fortified Jeremiah for the trials ahead of him with words of encouragement and a promise of protection:

Get ready, Jeremiah; go and tell them everything I command you to say. Do not be afraid of them now, or I will make you even more afraid when you are with them. Listen, Jeremiah! Everyone in this land - the kings of Judah, the officials, the priests and the people - will be against you. But today I am giving

> *you the strength to resist them; you will be like a fortified city, an iron pillar, and a bronze wall. They will not defeat you, for I will be with you to protect you. I, the Lord, have spoken. (Jeremiah 1:17-19)*

Buoyed by the Lord's promise, Jeremiah set out, albeit uncomfortably. His message to the people of Judah was expressed in three parts, three messages that he presented concurrently and repeatedly. First, he called the people to repentance for their idolatry and sinful ways, but promised that contrition and repentance could spare them from judgment. Second, after they failed to heed his message and turn away from evil, he told them that their punishment was now unavoidable - that God would use the Babylonians as His instruments of punishment and the people must surrender to them to escape utter destruction. And third, Jeremiah promised that God would ultimately forgive and restore His Chosen People, and establish a new and eternal covenant with them.

The Book of Jeremiah is comprised of 52 chapters. They tell the story of Jeremiah and present his messages and predictions, but the book is not composed in chronological order, so identifying a time frame to place each pronouncement in its proper context has proven to be quite difficult for Biblical scholars. Jeremiah's three main messages to Judah are, therefore, interspersed, rather than presented in a systematic or sequential order. Much of the Book of Jeremiah contains words that were dictated by Jeremiah to Baruch, a Temple scribe who became his secretary, companion and confidant. The Book of Jeremiah utilizes a variety of writing styles, both prosaic and poetic, that contribute to its richness and sense of passion. Jeremiah's predictions stand out because they are mostly written in verse rather than in straight prose.

Although Jeremiah received his prophetic call during King Josiah's reign, it appears that most of his pronouncements and ministerial activities occurred during the later reigns of Jehoiakim and Zedekiah (as the reigns of Jehoahaz - who was deposed - and Jehoiachin - who was exiled - were very short-lived). One of the reasons the people refused to heed Jeremiah's warnings was their strong belief that Jerusalem would never be overrun or threatened. They believed that

God would prevent that from happening since Jerusalem was home to the Temple, God's dwelling place. This view was strengthened years earlier by the death of 185,000 Assyrian soldiers as they prepared to invade Jerusalem during the reign of their emperor Sennacherib. This was an attitude that needed to be shattered, and the Lord sent Jeremiah to decry it in a powerful speech that has come to be called the "Temple Sermon":

> *"The Lord sent me to the gate of the Temple where the people of Judah went in to worship. He told me to stand there and announce what the Lord Almighty, the God of Israel, had to say to them: "Change the way you are living and the things you are doing, and I will let you go on living here. Stop believing those deceitful words, 'We are safe. This is the Lord's Temple, this is the Lord's Temple, this is the Lord's Temple!'*
>
> *Change the way you are living and stop doing the things you are doing. Be fair in your treatment of one another. Stop taking advantage of aliens, orphans and widows. Stop killing innocent people in this land. Stop worshiping other gods, for that will destroy you. If you change, I will let you go on living here in the land which I gave your ancestors as a permanent possession.*
>
> *Look, you put your trust in deceitful words. You steal, murder, commit adultery, tell lies under oath, offer sacrifices to Baal, and worship gods that you had not known before. You do these things I hate, and then you come and stand in My presence, in My own Temple, and say, 'We are safe!' Do you think that My Temple is a hiding place for robbers? I have seen what you are doing. Go to Shiloh, the first place where I chose to be worshiped, and see what I did to it because of the sins of My people Israel. You have committed all these sins, and even though I spoke to you over and over again, you refused to listen. You would not answer when I called you. And so, what I did to Shiloh I will do to this Temple of Mine, in which you trust....I will drive you out of My sight as I drove out your relatives, the people of Israel. I, the Lord, have spoken." (Jeremiah 7:1-15)*

When Jeremiah was finished speaking, the crowd that had assembled at the Temple was outraged. They wanted to put Jeremiah to death for speaking against the city. But Jeremiah repeated his warning to King

Jehoiakim and the leaders of Jerusalem when they arrived on the scene, reminding them that it was not too late to avoid destruction:

> *The Lord sent me to proclaim everything that you heard me say against this Temple and against this city. You must change the way you are living and the things you are doing, and must obey the Lord your God. If you do, He will change His mind about the destruction that He said He would bring on you. As for me, I am in your power! Do with me whatever you think is fair and right. But be sure of this: if you kill me, you and the people of this city will be guilty of killing an innocent man, because it is the Lord who sent me to give you this warning. (Jeremiah 26:12-15)*

Realizing that Jeremiah had spoken in the name of God, and remembering that the prophet Micah had also previously foretold of the destruction of Jerusalem, Jehoiakim chose not to punish Jeremiah - on this one occasion - other than to ban him from the Temple. But neither did the king nor the people of Jerusalem listen to his words, accept his advice or change their ways to prevent future destruction. Jeremiah was either ignored, ridiculed or insulted. Rather naive, he was also shocked to discover a plot against his life by men from his own village of Anathoth. As a result, God again offered reassurance to Jeremiah:

> *They will fight against you, but they will not defeat you. I will be with you to protect you and keep you safe. I will rescue you from the power of wicked and violent men. I, the Lord, have spoken. (Jeremiah 15:20-21)*

God also imposed other restrictions on Jeremiah. Unlike the prophet Hosea, who was told by God to marry a prostitute who would be unfaithful to him, Jeremiah was told by God that he was not to marry or have children - that the women and children would die either by disease, warfare or starvation. Similarly, he was instructed not to enter the home of anyone in mourning or to grieve with or for anyone. This represented God's lack of pity for all those who chose the path of infidelity to Him.

The Lord instructed Jeremiah to visit the home of a potter in order to deliver His message:

> So I went there and saw the potter working at his wheel. Whenever a piece of pottery turned out imperfect, he would take the clay and make it into something else. Then the Lord said to me, "Don't I have the right to do with you people of Israel what the potter did with the clay? You are in My hands just like clay in the potter's hands. If at any time I say that I am going to uproot, break down, or destroy any nation or kingdom, but then that nation turns from its evil, I will not do what I said I would. On the other hand, if I say that I am going to plant or build up any nation or kingdom, but then that nation disobeys Me or does evil, I will not do what I said I would. Now then, tell the people of Judah and of Jerusalem that I am making plans against them and getting ready to punish them. Tell them to stop living sinful lives - to change their ways and the things they are doing. They will answer, 'No, why should we? We will all be just as stubborn and as evil as we want to be.'" (Jeremiah 18:3-12)

The Lord also instructed Jeremiah to buy a clay jar and bring some of the priests and elders to Hinnom Valley, where the people had constructed altars to Baal and sacrificed their own children as offerings. Through Jeremiah the Lord promised:

> ...the time will come when this place will no longer be called...Himmon Valley.
>
> Instead it will be called Slaughter Valley. In this place I will frustrate the plans of the people of Judah and Jerusalem. I will let their enemies triumph over them and kill them in battle. I will give their corpses to the birds and the wild animals as food.
>
> I will bring such terrible destruction on this city that everyone who passes by will be shocked and amazed. The enemy will surround the city and try to kill its people.
>
> The siege will be so terrible that the people inside the city will eat one another and even their own children. Then the Lord told me to break the jar in front of the men...and tell them "I will break this people and this city, and it will be like this broken clay jar that cannot be put together again." (Jeremiah 19:6-11)

When Jeremiah's proclamations reached the ear of Pashhur, the chief officer of the Temple, Pashhur had Jeremiah beaten and chained at the Temple. Jeremiah's frustration got the best of him, and he complained to the Lord:

> *Everyone makes fun of me; they laugh at me all day long...Lord, I am ridiculed and scorned all the time because I proclaim Your message...I hear everyone whispering..."Let's report him to the authorities!" Even my close friends wait for my downfall... "Perhaps...we can catch him and get revenge."...Curse the day I was born...Why was I born? Was it only to have trouble and sorrow, to end my life in disgrace? (Jeremiah 20:7-8,10,14,18)*

Yet, Jeremiah's sufferings and disillusionment were far from over. In the fourth year of the reign of King Jehoiakim, circa 605 BCE, and the first year of the reign of King Nebuchadnezzar of Babylon, the Lord gave Jeremiah a message to deliver to all the people of Judah:

> *For twenty-three years...the Lord has spoken to me, and I have never failed to tell you what He said. But you have paid no attention. You would not listen...even though the Lord has continued to send you His servants the prophets. They told you to turn from your wicked way of life and from the evil things you are doing, so that you could go on living in the land that the Lord gave you and your ancestors as a permanent possession. They told you not to worship and serve other gods and not to make the Lord angry by worshiping the idols you had made. If you had obeyed the Lord, then He would not have punished you. But the Lord Himself says that you refused to listen to Him. Instead, you made Him angry with your idols and have brought His punishment on yourselves.*
>
> *So then, because you would not listen to Him, the Lord Almighty says, "I am going to send for all the peoples from the north and for My servant, King Nebuchadnezzar of Babylonia. I am going to bring them to fight against Judah and its inhabitants...I am going to destroy this nation...This whole land will be left in ruins and will be a shocking sight, and...serve the king of Babylonia for seventy years. After that I will punish Babylonia and its king for their sin. I will destroy that country and leave it in ruins forever." (Jeremiah 25:3-13)*

Nebuchadnezzar was both ruthless and strategic. No sooner had he ascended to the throne of Babylon than Nebuchadnezzar captured Jerusalem and took hostages from among its nobility to keep King Jehoiakim from reneging on his oath of loyalty as a vassal. Daniel (who will be discussed more fully in Chapter 12), Michael, Azariah and Hananiah were among the hostages taken at this time. Several years later, when Jehoiakim - thinking that Babylon had grown weaker - switched his allegiance to Egypt, he ignored the warning of Jeremiah, who encouraged him to trust in the Lord rather than in political alliances. Since Jehoiakim had banned Jeremiah from the Temple, to convey God's messages to the people, Jeremiah asked Baruch, a Temple scribe who had joined him as a secretary and disciple, to write out God's message onto a scroll and read it at the Temple. After Baruch had done this, he was brought to the royal palace, where he read Jeremiah's words to a group of court officials, who, in turn, brought the scroll to King Jehoiakim. The king burned the scroll and sent men to arrest Jeremiah and Baruch, but they concealed themselves and escaped capture.

Nebuchadnezzar returned in 597 BCE to invade Judah and lay siege to Jerusalem. Jehoiakim died (it's not known whether he died in Jerusalem or if he was captured - and died in Babylon), and his teenage son Jehoiachin ascended to the throne. He relinquished his throne to Nebuchadnezzar within several months to save Jerusalem from destruction, and was exiled to Babylon with his family and a large number of Judah's officials, artisans and skilled craftsmen. Included in this group of deportees was the priest and prophet Ezekiel. All of them would toil in service to Babylon. It was largely the lower class poor of Jerusalem who remained, and Nebuchadnezzar appointed Jehoiachin's uncle Mattaniah to rule Judea as a puppet king, vassal to Babylon. Mattaniah's name was changed to Zedekiah, and Jeremiah, who remained in Jerusalem, would now be delivering God's pronouncements to him.

Shortly after Zedekiah had been named king, the Lord instructed Jeremiah to construct a yoke out of leather straps and wooden bars and wear it around his neck as a symbol of submission. Jeremiah was then to make a pronouncement to the ambassadors from Edom, Moab, Ammon, Tyre and Sidon who were visiting Zedekiah at the time that it was only through submission to Babylon that they could avoid utter destruction.

> *The Lord Almighty, the God of Israel, told me… "By My great power and strength I created the world, mankind, and all the animals that live on the earth; and I give it to anyone I choose. I am the One Who has placed all these nations under the power of My servant, King Nebuchadnezzar of Babylonia, and I have made even the wild animals serve him. All nations will serve him, and they will serve under his son and his grandson until the time comes for his own nation to fall….But if any nation or kingdom will not submit to his rule, then I will punish that nation by war, starvation, and disease until I have let Nebuchadnezzar destroy it completely. Do not listen to your prophets who…tell you not to submit to the king of Babylonia.*
>
> *They are deceiving you and will cause you to be taken far away from your country.*
>
> *I will drive you out, and you will be destroyed. But if any nation submits to the king of Babylonia and serves him, then I will let it stay on its own land, to farm it and live there. I, the Lord, have spoken." (Jeremiah 27:5-11)*

He had essentially the same message to deliver specifically to King Zedekiah:

> *I said the same thing to King Zedekiah of Judah. Submit to the king of Babylonia.*
>
> *Serve him and his people and you will live. Why should you and your people die in war or of starvation or disease? That is what the Lord has said will happen to any nation that does not submit to the king of Babylonia. Do not listen to the prophets who tell you not to surrender to him. They are deceiving you. The Lord Himself has said that He did not send them and that they are lying to you in His Name. And so He will drive you out, and you will be killed, you and the prophets who are telling you these lies. (Jeremiah 27:12-15)*

It was after these pronouncements that a false prophet by the name of Hananiah from the town of Gibeon addressed the assemblage. He told them that the Lord and spoken to him and said:

> I have broken the power of the king of Babylonia. Within two years I will bring back to this place all the Temple treasures that King Nebuchadnezzar took to Babylonia. I will also bring back the king of Judah, Jehoiachin, son of Jehoiakim, along with all of the people of Judah who went into exile...I, the Lord, have spoken. (Jeremiah 28:2-4)

Hananiah then removed the yoke from around Jeremiah's neck and broke it, saying:

> The Lord has said that this is how he will break the yoke that King Nebuchadnezzar has put on the neck of all the nations; and He will do this within two years. (Jeremiah 28:10-11)

Jeremiah responded to Hananiah:

> The Lord has said that you may be able to break a wooden yoke, but He will replace it with an iron yoke...all these nations...will serve King Nebuchadnezzar...Listen, Hananiah! The Lord did not send you, and you are making these people believe a lie. And so the Lord Himself says that He is going to get rid of you. Before this year is over you will die because you have told the people to rebel against the Lord. (Jeremiah 28:12-16)

Hananiah died in the seventh month of that same year.

After a time, Zedekiah, as Jehoiakim had done previously, wanted to throw off the yoke of Babylonian tyranny. He sought to align Judah with Egypt, but Jeremiah discouraged him from this alliance. He told Zedekiah:

> The Egyptian army is on its way to help you, but it will return home. Then the Babylonians will come back, attack the city, capture it, and burn it down. (Jeremiah 37:7-8)

As Jeremiah left Jerusalem to return to his home in Anathoth, he was accused of desertion at the city gates and imprisoned in an underground cell for "a long time." When Jeremiah was eventually summoned by Zedekiah, he asked the king what crimes he had committed that were worthy of imprisonment, but he remained a prisoner, even though his incarceration was transferred to the palace courtyard from his underground cell.

Several palace officials, troubled by Jeremiah's pronouncements that the people of Judea must submit to the Babylonians or be killed, demanded of the king that Jeremiah be put to death.

> By talking like this he is making the soldiers in the city lose their courage, and he is doing the same to everyone else left in the city. He is not trying to help the people; he only wants to hurt them. (Jeremiah 38:4)

Zedekiah let them have their way, so they lowered Jeremiah into a cistern in the palace courtyard, expecting him to die of thirst and starvation.

When an Ethiopian eunuch named Ebedmelech saw this, he begged the king to rescind the order. The king permitted Jeremiah to be raised from the cistern and returned to the palace courtyard. Later, Zedekiah summoned Jeremiah to ask for his advice. Jeremiah told him:

> ...the Lord Almighty, the God of Israel...said, "If you surrender to the king of Babylonia's officers, your life will be spared, and this city will not be burned down. Both you and your family will be spared. But if you do not surrender, then this city will be handed over to the Babylonians, who will burn it down, and you will not escape from them"...I beg you to obey the Lord's message... (Jeremiah 38:17-20)

Jeremiah was imprisoned again, and Nebuchadnezzar's forces attacked Jerusalem. When they broke through the city walls, Zedekiah did not surrender to the Babylonian officials. He tried to sneak out with his family and close advisors during the night, but was captured by the Babylonian army and brought before Nebuchadnezzar. While

Zedekiah looked on, Nebuchadnezzar put to death all of Zedekiah's sons and advisors. Nebuchadnezzar then had Zedekiah blinded, put in chains and brought to Babylon to become a slave. Meanwhile, Jerusalem was burned to the ground and its people taken away as prisoners to Babylon. Only the poorest of the poor were left behind.

Nebuchadnezzar also instructed Nebuzaradan, the commander of his army, to find Jeremiah and treat him with respect. When he found that Jeremiah had been incarcerated, he released him and permitted him to accompany the other Judeans to Babylon or choose to go elsewhere. Nebuchadnezzar appointed Gedaliah, the grandson of a former secretary of the Judean court, to serve as his governor in Judah, and Jeremiah chose to remain with him in the town of Mizpah, several miles north of Jerusalem. Gedaliah's appointment encouraged some Judean farmers who had fled the Babylonian invasion to return to their homeland to plant crops and vines, but there were other Judean soldiers who had never capitulated to the Babylonians. One of them, Ishmael, the son of Nethaniah, assassinated Gedaliah and many of his officers and followers and took other followers of Gedaliah as prisoners. Ishmael, in turn, was hunted and killed by other soldiers under the command of Johanan, the son of Kareah, but Johanan and all the people he saved from Ishmael were afraid of the Babylonians, who would be angry that King Nebuchadnezzar's appointed governor had been killed. Even though they were innocent of this bloodshed, they made plans to flee to Egypt.

Before embarking for Egypt, this group of Judeans asked Jeremiah to pray to the Lord for guidance and instruction, promising to do whatever the Lord commanded.

> *Whether it pleases us or not, we will obey the Lord our God, to Whom we are asking you to pray. All will go well with us if we obey Him. (Jeremiah 42:6)*

After ten days, Jeremiah delivered the Lord's message to Johanan and his fellow Judeans.

> *The Lord, the God of Israel...has said "If you are willing to go on living in this land, then I will build you up and not tear you down...but...you must not say, 'No, we will go and live in Egypt, where we won't face war anymore...or go hungry'...If you are determined to go and live in Egypt, then the war that you fear will overtake you, and the hunger you dread will follow you, and you will die there in Egypt...My fury will be poured out on you if you go to Egypt." (Jeremiah 42:10,13-16,18)*

Amazingly, the Judeans did not believe Jeremiah. Their response to him was:

> *You are lying. The Lord our God did not send you to tell us not to go and live in Egypt. Baruch...has stirred you up against us, so that the Babylonians will gain power over us and...either kill us or take us away to Babylonia. (Jeremiah 43:2-3)*

So they disregarded the Lord's command and emigrated to Egypt, taking a protesting Jeremiah and Baruch with them.

Upon their arrival in the city of Tahpanhes, the Lord told Jeremiah:

> *Get some large stones and bury them...in front of...the government building...and let some of the Israelites see you do it. Then tell them that I, the Lord Almighty, the God of Israel, am going to bring My servant King Nebuchadnezzar of Babylonia to this place, and he will put his throne over these stones...Nebuchadnezzar will come and defeat Egypt. Those people who are doomed to die of disease will die of disease, those doomed to be taken away as prisoners will be taken away as prisoners, and those doomed to be killed in war will be killed in war. (Jeremiah 43:9-11)*

The Lord went on to say more specifically:

> *As for the people of Judah who are...determined to...live in Egypt, I will see to it that all of them are destroyed. All of them, great and small, will die in Egypt, either in war or of starvation. (Jeremiah 44:12)*

And the rest of Jeremiah's personal story is clouded in the mists of history. The extent to which Nebuchadnezzar defeated the Egyptians and staked a claim on Egyptian territory is debated by historians. Portions of Egyptian history composed during this era by Egyptian priests may have "soft-pedaled" the inroads made by Babylonian forces into their territory. And nothing further is mentioned of Jeremiah - how much longer he lived, how he died, if he remained in Egypt for his remaining years. Dr. Charles H. Dyer of the Moody Bible Institute in Chicago described Jeremiah as "the premier prophet of Judah during the dark days leading to her destruction...Jeremiah was the blazing torch who, along with Ezekiel in Babylon, exposed the darkness of Judah's sin with the piercing brightness of God's Word. He was a weeping prophet to a wayward people."

As mentioned earlier, the three primary messages of Jeremiah are repeated and repeated throughout the 52 chapters of the Book of Jeremiah as well as in the Book of Lamentations, which is usually considered to be the work of Jeremiah as well. Below are yet several more examples of these messages that "dot the landscape of Jeremiah" in maddening disarray.

A CALL TO REPENTANCE

Jeremiah began his ministry with an urgent plea to the people of Judah to recognize and affirm their sinful ways - especially as it applies to their penchant for idolatry. And they must repent. He said,

> Then the Lord told me ...to say to Israel, "Unfaithful Israel, come back to Me. I am merciful and will not be angry with you forever. Only admit that you are guilty and that you have rebelled against the Lord, your God. Confess that under every green tree you have given your love to foreign gods and that you have not obeyed My commands." (Jeremiah 3:11-13)

Again Jeremiah affirmed that it was not too late to repent and be saved.

> *Jerusalem, wash the evil from your heart, so that you may be saved. (Jeremiah 4:14)*

God's forgiveness is so gracious that He will show His mercy even with a token acknowledgment of righteousness.

> *People of Jerusalem, run through your streets! Look around! See for yourselves! Search the marketplaces! Can you find one person who does what is right and tries to be faithful to God? If you can, the Lord will forgive Jerusalem. (Jeremiah 5:1)*

THE INEVITABILITY OF PUNISHMENT

Failure to admit sinfulness - much less to take steps to turn away from it - must necessarily result in punishment. Over the course of time, Jeremiah's predictions about God's upcoming retribution became more and more specific. Through Jeremiah, the Lord spoke:

> *...You say, "I am innocent; surely the Lord is no longer angry with me." But I, the Lord, will punish you because you deny that you have sinned. You have cheapened yourself by turning to the gods of other nations. You will be disappointed by Egypt, just as you were by Assyria...You will not gain anything from them. (Jeremiah 2:35-37)*

More specifically, and with great urgency, Jeremiah continued to warn the people.

> *Run for safety! Don't delay! The Lord is bringing disaster and great destruction from the north. Like a lion coming from its hiding place, a destroyer of nations has set out. He is coming to destroy Judah. The cities of Judah will be left in ruins, and no one will live in them. So put on sackcloth and weep and wail because the fierce anger of the Lord has not turned away from Judah. (Jeremiah 4:6-8)*

> *The people of Jerusalem not only refused to believe in Jeremiah's predictions of future destruction and Exile, but they taunted Jeremiah: "The people say to*

me, 'Where are those threats the Lord made against us? Let Him carry them out now!" (Jeremiah 17:15)

THE PROMISE OF RESTORATION

The dark days are only temporary, but hopefully a valuable lesson in fidelity will have been learned, proper punishment for transgressions will have been meted, and a new era will finally begin.

> *The Lord says, "When Babylon's seventy years are over, I will show My concern for you and keep My promise to bring you back home. I alone know the plans I have for you, plans to bring you prosperity and not disaster...I will restore you to your land. I will gather you from every country...to which I have scattered you...I, the Lord, have spoken." (Jeremiah 29:10-14)*

> *I will heal this city [Jerusalem] and its people and restore them to health. I will show them abundant peace and security. I will make Judah and Israel prosperous, and I will rebuild them as they were before. (Jeremiah 33:6-7)*

> *...I will bring you back to Mount Zion. I will give you rulers who obey Me, and they will rule you with wisdom and understanding....When that time comes, Jerusalem will be called "The Throne of the Lord" and all nations will gather there to worship Me....Israel will join with Judah, and together they will come from exile in the country in the north and will return to the land that I gave your ancestors as a permanent possession. (Jeremiah 3:14-18)*

Perhaps the single most famous and most dramatic promise of restoration from the Book of Jeremiah is the best summary of his life's pronouncements to the people of Judah from their God - the God Who always loved them:

> *The Lord says, "The time is coming when I will make a new covenant with the people of Israel and with the people of Judah. It will not be like the old covenant I made with their ancestors when I took them by the hand and led them out of Egypt...The new covenant I make with the people of Israel will be this: I will put My law within them and write it on their hearts. I will be their God, and they will be My people." (Jeremiah 31:31-33)*

CHAPTER 11: QUESTIONS FOR REVIEW

1. Where and when was Jeremiah born? What is known of his family life?
2. How was Jeremiah called by God to his ministry?
3. What was the purpose of the two visions Jeremiah experienced - the almond tree and the overturned pot?
4. For what reason has Jeremiah been nicknamed "the reluctant prophet?"
5. What were the three dominant messages that Jeremiah preached to the people of Judea?
6. What is it about the Book of Jeremiah that makes it difficult to follow?
7. What was King Jehoiakim's reaction to Jeremiah's "Temple Sermon?"
8. Why was Jeremiah instructed by God neither to grieve nor to marry?
9. Who was Baruch, and what was his relationship with Jeremiah?
10. Why did King Zedekiah side with Hananiah against Jeremiah?
11. Why did the people of Jerusalem view Jeremiah as both a coward and a traitor?

12. What did Jeremiah predict would happen to Zedekiah at the hands of the Babylonians?
13. What happened to Jeremiah after Nebuchadnezzar burned Jerusalem to the ground?

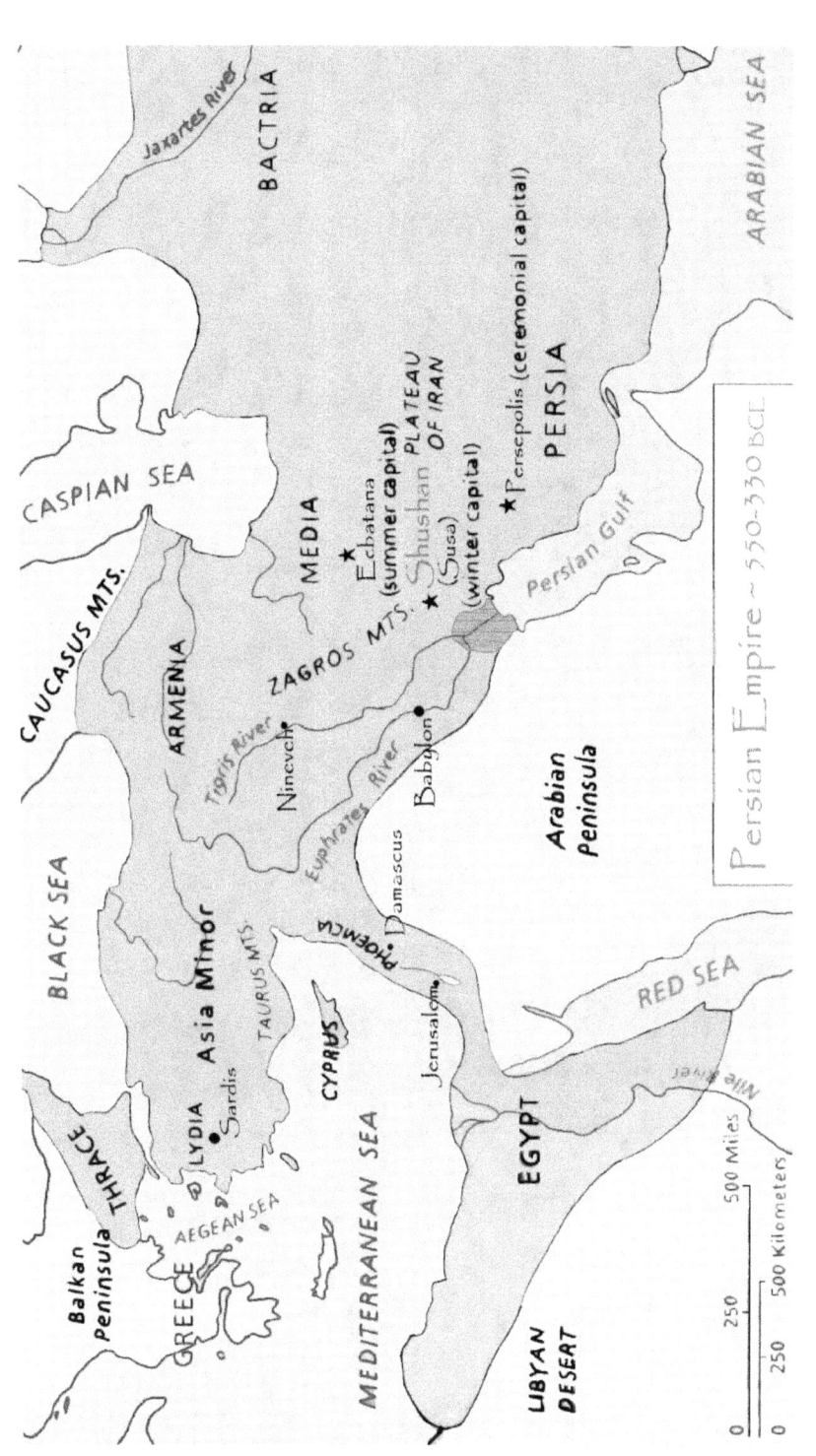

Chapter Twelve
DANIEL

"You have been weighed on the scales and found to be too light"

The popular Elton John song "Daniel" was not written about the prophet with the same name, but the lyric "I can see Daniel waving goodbye" certainly applies to the prophet's experience. If one accepts the premise that, while all prophets share a common ministry, they lived very different individual lives with unique circumstances, then the fact that Daniel experienced his call from God while serving as a hostage in the court of the Babylonian king Nebuchadnezzar has to stand out as a truly unique experience.

Daniel is one of the better known figures in the Old Testament, and while the Book of Daniel was not listed among the *Neviim* (Prophetic Books) of the Hebrew Scriptures, Daniel is nevertheless regarded as an authentic prophet as earmarked by his relationship with God as well as with the dreams and visions he either experienced or interpreted. While his upcoming escape from the lions' den is the most well-known and oft-repeated episode in his life, it is really his gift for dream interpretation (not unlike that of Joseph in pre-Exodus Egypt) and his predictions of future global dynasties that really seal his status as a prophet.

HOSTAGES, TRAINEES AND COURTIERS

Nebuchadnezzar's rise to power in Babylon demonstrated not only his thirst for power and domination, as well as his ruthlessness and greed, but also his political savvy and capacity for long-term planning. When Nebuchadnezzar's forces captured Jerusalem in 605 BCE (which was the third year in the reign of Judah's King Jehoiakim), he instructed his chief official Ashpenaz to have his soldiers carry off several teenaged members of Jewish nobility.

> *They had to be handsome, intelligent, well-trained, quick to learn, and free from physical defects. (Daniel 1:4)*

Daniel and his friends Hananiah, Mishael and Azariah met these criteria and were to be trained to serve as chamberlains in Nebuchadnezzar's court. Their training in the Babylonian language and culture would not only enrich the court, but make them valuable hostages to keep Jehoiakim and his allies from attempting an insurrection against Babylon.

The Judean hostages were recognized immediately upon their admittance into the Babylonian court for their wisdom and breeding. Daniel emerged as their leader, and demonstrated an even higher capacity for erudition. To indoctrinate the four more fully into the Babylonian worldview, the names of Daniel and his three fellow hostages were changed to Babylonian appellations - Daniel became Belteshazzar, Hananiah became Shadrach, Mishael became Meshach and Azariah became Abednego. Attempts such as these to separate individuals from their past lives are used today by a number of what we now call "destructive cults," whether their orientation is religious, political or psychological. Yet, this plan to steer them away from their Judean roots was unsuccessful. It was the intention of Daniel and his friends to remain true to their God and to the religious and cultural practices of Judah. To this end, they immediately caused a controversy by their refusal to eat the foods that were prepared for them as members of Nebuchadnezzar's court. Because the preparations were not conducted under the stringent rules of Judaic dietary law and because the food may also have been used in sacrifices to the gods of Babylon, the food was considered to be "ritually impure" - and unfit for consumption. They requested permission to subsist exclusively on vegetables and water, a request that flew in the face of Babylonian protocol and could have been viewed as an affront to the king. Nevertheless, a kindly Ashpenaz granted their request - conditionally - and a crisis was averted.

Daniel and his comrades trained under the guidance of Ashpenaz for three years before making their first appearance before Nebuchadnezzar, who was immediately impressed with them.

> *No matter what question the king asked or what problem he raised, these four knew ten times more than any fortune teller or magician in his whole kingdom. (Daniel 1:20)*

However, a positive first impression notwithstanding, Daniel and his friends found their lives threatened by Nebuchadnezzar's wrath on more than one occasion.

NEBUCHADNEZZAR'S DREAM

Very early in Nebuchadnezzar's reign, shortly after Daniel and his friends had concluded their courtly training and entered the service of the king as his advisors, the king was troubled by a nightmare that both frightened and confused him. This scenario is very reminiscent of the nightmare that troubled Pharaoh in the time after Joseph was sold into slavery in Egypt. But here the similarity ends. While Pharaoh explained his dream to Joseph in the hope that Joseph could offer an appropriate interpretation, Nebuchadnezzar approached the same situation from a very different angle.

Nebuchadnezzar summoned all of his advisors before him and demanded an interpretation of his dream. When they asked him to explain the details of the dream, Nebuchadnezzar balked.

> *The king said to them, "I have made up my mind that you must tell me the dream and then tell me what it means. If you can't, I'll have you torn limb from limb and make your house a pile of ruins...Tell me what the dream was, and then I will know that you can also tell me what it means." (Daniel 2:5,9)*

When the king's advisors - his fortune tellers, wizards and magicians - told him that such a feat would be impossible, the king ordered the execution of all of his advisors. Although Daniel, Hananiah, Mishael and Azariah were not present, the king's order applied to all of his advisors, including these four from Judah.

Daniel obtained permission for a little more time to enable him to tell Nebuchadnezzar both the contents of his dream as well as its interpretation. He enlisted his friends to pray to God with him to reveal the dream and its meaning, and later than night, the mystery was revealed to Daniel in a vision from God.

DANIEL • 177

In the morning, Daniel begged the executioner to stay his hand while Daniel explained the king's dream to Nebuchadnezzar. He told the king:

> Your Majesty, there is no wizard, magician, fortune teller or astrologer who can tell you... but there is a God in heaven who reveals mysteries. He has informed Your Majesty what will happen in the future. Now I will tell you the dream, the vision you had while you were asleep...Your Majesty, in your vision you saw standing before you a giant statue, bright and shining, and terrifying to look at. Its head was made of the finest gold, its chest and arms were made of silver, its waist and hips of bronze, its legs of iron, and its feet partly of iron and partly of clay. While you were looking at it, a great stone broke loose from a cliff without anyone touching it, struck the iron and clay feet of the statue, and shattered them. At once the iron, clay, bronze, silver and gold crumbled and became like the dust...The wind carried it all away, leaving not a trace. But the stone grew to be a mountain that covered the whole earth. (Daniel 2:27-35)

Daniel went on to explain the meaning of this dream that had been so troublesome and frightening to Nebuchadnezzar:

> Your Majesty, you are the greatest of all kings. The God of heaven has made you emperor and given you power, might and honor. He has made you ruler of all the inhabited earth and ruler over all the animals and birds. You are the head of gold. After you there will be another empire, not as great as yours, and after that a third, an empire of bronze, which will rule the whole world. And then there will be a fourth empire, as strong as iron, which shatters and breaks everything...And just as iron shatters everything, it will shatter and crush all the earlier empires. You also saw that the feet and the toes were partly clay and partly iron. This means that it will be a divided empire. It will have something of the strength of iron, because there was iron mixed with the clay. The toes - partly iron and partly clay - mean that part of the empire will be strong and part of it weak. You also saw that the iron was mixed with the clay.

> This means that the rulers of the empire will try to unite their families by intermarriage, but they will not be able to, any more than iron can mix with clay. At the time of those rulers the God of heaven will establish a kingdom

> that will never end. It will never be conquered, but will completely destroy all those empires and then last forever. You saw how a stone broke loose from a cliff without anyone touching it and how it struck the statue made of iron, bronze, clay silver and gold. The great God is telling Your Majesty what will happen in the future. I have told you exactly what you dreamed, and have given you its meaning. (Daniel 2:37-45)

After hearing Daniel's interpretation, Nebuchadnezzar acknowledged that Daniel's God is

> ….the greatest of all gods, the Lord over kings, and the one who reveals mysteries. (Daniel 2:47)

He then offered gifts to Daniel and appointed him and his three Judean comrades to important administrative positions. Daniel himself was placed in charge of the province of Babylon as well as all of the royal advisers.

It should be noted that Biblical scholars such as Dr. J. Dwight Pentecost (*The Bible Knowledge Commentary: Major Prophets*, (2018) believe that the four distinct metals used in the statue in Nebuchadnezzar's dream foreshadow several other empires that were destined to supplant Babylon. If Babylon is represented by the head of gold, then the chest and arms of silver would seem to represent the Persian Empire, the waist and hips of bronze would symbolize the Greeks, and the legs of iron would foreshadow the Roman Empire. It is unknown whether it dawned on Nebuchadnezzar that Daniel's God had bestowed a rich and singular blessing on him - granting Nebuchadnezzar the privilege of glimpsing the future to see the unveiling of God's Divine Plan.

THE FIERY FURNACE

In the court of Nebuchadnezzar, it was possible for fortunes to change overnight, and the accolades accorded to Daniel, Hananiah (Shadrach), Mishael (Meshach) and Azariah (Abednego) could - and did - dissipate rapidly. The tale of the "fiery furnace" is proof positive, but it centers around Daniel's friends rather than Daniel. The saga began when

Nebuchadnezzar authorized the construction of a 90-foot golden statue, which was dedicated in an elaborate ceremony on the plain of Dura in the province of Babylon. All of Nebuchadnezzar's officials were ordered to attend the ceremony, where they would be required at the proper moment to bow down before the statue and worship it. It is unclear why Daniel was not present at these festivities, but his three friends were in attendance - and refused to prostrate themselves before the statue. When apprised of this act of defiance, Nebuchadnezzar threatened to throw the three into a fiery furnace (most probably a large kiln for use in making pottery) if they refused to comply. Their response (pardon the pun) only fanned the flames:

> *Your Majesty, we will not try to defend ourselves. If the God Whom we serve is able to save us from the blazing furnace and from your power, then He will. But even if He doesn't, Your Majesty may be sure that we will not worship your god, and we will not bow down to the gold statue that you have set up.* (Daniel 3:16-18)

An infuriated Nebuchadnezzar had Hananiah, Mishael and Azariah bound and thrown into a furnace, after demanding that its heat be increased dramatically. He asked his victims with sarcasm and arrogance:

> *Do you think there is any god who can save you?* (Daniel 3:15)

After they were thrown into the furnace, whose flames were so intense that they burned the guards who threw them there, Nebuchadnezzar was astounded to see that the three were no longer bound, that they were walking freely among the flames without any fear or danger to themselves, and were accompanied by a fourth man

> *...who looks like an angel.* (Daniel 3:25)

Nebuchadnezzar was both dumbfounded and humbled. He reversed himself completely, saying,

> *Praise the God of Shadrach, Meshach and Abednego! He sent His angel and rescued these men who serve and trust Him. They disobeyed my orders and risked their lives rather than bow down and worship any god except their own. And now I command that if anyone of any nation, race or language speaks disrespectfully of the God of Shadrach, Meshach and Abednego, he is to be torn limb from limb, and his house is to be made a pile of ruins. There is no other God Who can rescue like this. (Daniel 3:29)*

The salvific power displayed by Yahweh in His protection of the three Judeans in the fiery furnace, as well as Daniel's interpretation of Nebuchadnezzar's dream as provided by Yahweh, were designed to show Nebuchadnezzar that the power of Yahweh is supreme, and that Nebuchadnezzar's conquest of Judah was by God's design and purpose. Nebuchadnezzar was but a tool used by God for His own purposes. He was allowed to usurp Judah and even massacre a large number of Judeans because that was ordained and permitted by Yahweh, yet Nebuchadnezzar could not even harm three youngsters in "his own backyard" because Yahweh would not, in turn, permit that. So where does true power really lie? J. Daniel Hays suggested in his *The Message of the Prophets* (2010), that the Book of Daniel makes one thing abundantly clear - that ultimate power rests with God, Who is able and willing to direct His Divine Plan through the activities of such empires as the Babylonians and Persians.

NEBUCHADNEZZAR'S SECOND DREAM

A lengthy period of time elapsed, during which it is quite possible that Nebuchadnezzar's arrogance only increased. So it happened that Nebuchadnezzar was again plagued with another nightmare that cried out for interpretation. In his own words, Nebuchadnezzar described the details of the dream:

> *While I was asleep, I had a vision of a huge tree in the middle of the earth. It grew bigger and bigger until it reached the sky and could be seen by everyone in the world. Its leaves were beautiful, and it was loaded down with fruit - enough for the whole world to eat. Wild animals rested in its*

shade, birds built nests in its branches, and every kind of living thing ate its fruit.

While I was thinking about the vision, I saw coming down from heaven an angel, alert and watchful. He proclaimed in a loud voice, "Cut the tree down and chop off its branches; strip off its leaves and scatter its fruit. Drive the animals from under it and the birds out of its branches. But leave the stump in the ground with a band of iron and bronze around it. Leave it there in the field with the grass. Now let the dew fall on this man, and let him live with the animals and plants. For seven years he will not have a human mind, but the mind of an animal. This is the decision of the alert and watchful angels. So then, let all people everywhere know that the Supreme God has power over human kingdoms and that He can give them to anyone He chooses - even to the least important of men." (Daniel 4:10-17)

For reasons unknown, Nebuchadnezzar did not immediately consult Daniel. It has been posited that the king may have suspected that the tree was a symbol for himself - trees were frequently used as representations of the reigning monarch, and in his dream, the king heard the angel refer to the tree as "the man" - and was initially embarrassed to summon Daniel. He may also have dreaded what he perceived to be a dire interpretation, and was hoping to forestall it. In either event, he was ultimately driven to call Daniel and request his interpretation. Over the years it is quite possible that a friendship had developed between Nebuchadnezzar and the advisor who had served him faithfully over the years, because it was with sincere regret that Daniel provided his interpretation of the symbolism.

Your Majesty, I wish that the dream and its explanation applied to your enemies and not to you...Your Majesty, you are the tree, tall and strong. You have grown so great that you reach the sky, and your power extends over the whole world...An angel came down from heaven and said, "Cut the tree down and destroy it, but leave the stump in the ground. Wrap a band of iron and bronze around it, and leave it there in the field... Let the dew fall on this man, and let him live there with the animals for seven years." This...is what it means...what the Supreme God has declared will happen to you. You will be driven away from human society and will live with wild animals. For seven

> years you will eat grass like an ox and sleep in the open air, where the dew will fall on you. Then you will admit that the Supreme God controls all human kingdoms and that He can give them to anyone He chooses. The angel ordered the stump to be left in the ground. This means that you will become king again when you acknowledge that God rules the world. (Daniel 4:19-26)

Nebuchadnezzar's foray into animalistic madness (known clinically as *zoanthropy*) did not begin until a year later. As he walked across the roof of his palace, complimenting himself on the glory of Babylon as well as his own might and majesty, he was silenced by a voice from heaven, which said,

> King Nebuchadnezzar, listen to what I say! Your royal power is now taken away from you. You will be driven away from human society, live with wild animals, and eat grass like an ox for seven years. Then you will acknowledge that the Supreme God has power over human kingdoms and that He can give them to anyone He chooses. (Daniel 4:31-32)

This sentence commenced immediately and lasted for the full seven years, during which time Nebuchadnezzar's hair grew long and the length of his fingernails made them look like bird claws. At the conclusion of the seven years, Nebuchadnezzar's sanity returned. In his own words...

> I looked up at the sky, and my sanity returned. I praised the Supreme God and gave honor and glory to the One Who lives forever. He will rule forever, and His kingdom will last for all time. He looks on the people of the earth as nothing; angels in heaven and people on earth are under His control. No one can oppose His will or question what He does. (Daniel 4:34-35)

Dr. James E. Smith, in his 1992 text *The Major Prophets*, outlined the completeness of the reversal of Nebuchadnezzar's fortunes: "As a result of his recognition of the rightful place of God, Nebuchadnezzar experienced a fourfold restoration. First, he was restored *mentally*...cured of the psychosis of zoanthropy. Second, he was restored *physically* - his 'majesty and splendor' returned. This would include his physical features and all the external trappings of kingship. Third, he was restored *politically*. Those who acted as regents during his incapacitation handed the reins of government back to Nebuchadnezzar....Fourth, he was restored *socially*. His counselors began to seek him out. Thus was Nebuchadnezzar's 'sovereignty' reestablished."

The question of whether or not Nebuchadnezzar experienced a complete, authentic conversion as a result of these experiences of the power of Yahweh remains unanswered. Yet, there can be no doubt that Daniel left an indelible imprint on the monarch who first captured him and then later came to rely heavily on his wisdom, his faith and devotion - and perhaps even his friendship.

Nebuchadnezzar died in 562 BCE and was succeeded by his son Amel Marduk, who was assassinated by his brother-in-law Neriglissar. Neriglissar died in 556 BCE and was succeeded by his son Labashi-Marduk, who reigned for only nine months. Nothing is known of the relationship between Daniel and these relatively short-lived monarchs or whether Daniel continued to hold the court position he held under Nebuchadnezzar. When Nabonidus ascended to the throne after toppling Labashi-Marduk, Daniel was now in his eighties.

The reign of Nabonidus introduced and included his son Belshazzar, who ruled with him as a co-regent. Nabonidus had earned the wrath of many Babylonians as a result of his devotion to the moon god, Sin, instead of to the chief Babylonian deity, Marduk. He also preferred to remain away from his capital for much of his reign, using his time and energy in the restoration and cataloging of religious relics - serving as the world's first recorded "archaeologist." This left the bulk of royal administration work to Belshazzar.

THE VISIONS OF THE FOUR BEASTS AND THE RAM AND GOAT

It was during the first year of Belshazzar's reign that Daniel experienced a dream, not unlike the much earlier dream of Nebuchadnezzar, that offered a glimpse into the distant future and the general sweep of human history. Daniel saw fit to write down the details of this dream when he awoke.

Winds were blowing from all directions and lashing the surface of the ocean. Four huge beasts came up out of the ocean, each one different from the others. The first one looked like a lion, but had wings like an eagle...The second beast looked like a bear standing on its hind legs. It was holding three ribs between its teeth, and a voice said to it, "Go on, eat as much meat as you can!"... Another beast appeared. It looked like a leopard, but on its back there were four wings, like the wings of a bird, and it had four heads. It had a look of authority about it...A fourth beast appeared. It was powerful, horrible, terrifying. With its huge iron teeth it crushed its victims, and then it trampled on them. Unlike the other beasts, it had ten horns.

While I was looking, thrones were put in place. One Who had been living forever sat down on one of the thrones. His clothes were white as snow, and His hair was like pure wool.

His throne, mounted on fiery wheels, was blazing with fire...As I watched, the fourth beast was killed, and its body was thrown into the flames and destroyed. The other beasts had their power taken away, but they were permitted to go on living for a limited time.

During this vision...I saw what looked like a human being....He went to the One Who had been living forever and was presented to Him. He was given authority, honor, and royal power, so that the people of all nations, races and languages would serve him. His authority would last forever, and his kingdom would never end. (Daniel 7:2-14)

It is a commonly accepted belief among most theologians that the imagery in Daniel's vision corresponds to the imagery in Nebuchadnezzar's dream, so ably interpreted by Daniel years earlier. In this case, each of the four beasts aligns with the four metals (and the empire each represents) of Nebuchadnezzar's statue: the lion with eagle's wings is the head of gold, representing the Babylonian Empire. The bear corresponds with the statue's chest and arms of silver, indicative of the Persian Empire and the winged leopard matches the waist of bronze and the Greek Empire. Finally, the terrifying fourth beast is the legs and feet of iron, representing the Roman Empire. When the scene shifts to the setting of thrones, clearly it is God Whose power and majesty overwhelm the "beastly" Empires, and the awaited Messiah Who is given final and perpetual authority over all of creation. However, it seems that Daniel did not realize the connection between this dream and the earlier dream of Nebuchadnezzar, nor did he comprehend the many symbols present in the dream, for he found it necessary to seek guidance:

> The visions I saw alarmed me, and I was deeply disturbed. I went up to one of those standing there [an angel] and asked him to explain it all. So he told me the meaning. (Daniel 7:15-16)

This vision of Daniel's also affirms the special place he is accorded within the prophetic tradition. Not only was he empowered to interpret the dream that allowed Nebuchadnezzar a glimpse into history, but now, with different imagery, Daniel is gifted with the same divinely-inspired worldview.

Approximately two years later, still within the reign of King Belshazzar, Daniel was puzzled by yet another vision:

> I found myself in the...city of Susa...standing by the Ulai River, and there beside the river I saw a ram that had two long horns...I watched the ram butting with his horns to the west, the north and the south. No animal could stop him...He did as he pleased and grew arrogant.
>
> While I was wondering what this meant, a goat came rushing out of the west, moving so fast that his feet didn't touch the ground. He had one prominent horn between his eyes...I watched him attack the ram...He smashed into him and broke the two horns. The ram had no strength to resist. He was thrown to the ground and trampled on, and there was no one who could save him.
>
> The goat grew more and more arrogant, but at the height of his power his horn was broken. In its place four prominent horns came up, each pointing in a different direction. Out of one of these four horns grew a little horn whose power extended to the south and the east and toward the Promised Land. It grew strong enough to attack the army of heaven...It even defied the Prince of the heavenly army, stopped the daily sacrifices offered to him, and ruined the Temple... (Daniel 8:2-11)

Again, Daniel admitted to being perplexed by the details of this vision, and again, its message is clarified through the intercession of a celestial advisor:

> *"I was trying to understand what the vision meant, when...I heard a voice call out... "Gabriel, explain to him the meaning of what he saw." Gabriel...stood beside me, and I was so terrified that I fell to the ground. He said, "Mortal man...I am showing you what the result of God's anger will be. The vision refers to the time of the end.*
>
> *The ram you saw that had two horns represents the kingdoms of Media and Persia.*
>
> *The goat represents the kingdom of Greece, and the prominent horn between his eyes is the first king. The four horns...represent the four kingdoms into which that nation will be divided and which will not be as strong as the first kingdom.*
>
> *When the end of those kingdoms is near...there will be a stubborn, vicious and deceitful king. He will grow strong...he will cause terrible destruction...He will even defy the greatest King of all, but he will be destroyed without the use of any human power. This vision...explained to you will come true. But keep it secret now, because it will be a long time before it does come true." (Daniel 8:17-26)*

While the symbols of the ram and goat are explicitly identified by Gabriel, Biblical scholars consistently identify the goat's horn (the "first king") as Alexander the Great and the second "stubborn, vicious and deceitful king" as Antiochus IV Epiphanes, who desecrated the Temple of Solomon with a statue of Zeus in the mid-second century BCE and attempted to bully the Judeans into worship of the Greek pantheon. Daniel's reaction to this revelation was physical, emotional and psychological - he became both physically ill for several days, lapsed into a temporary depression, and remained puzzled and confused by the details of the vision.

Several years passed in the reign of King Belshazzar, and it was at this time that the Persian Empire to the northeast had grown in power and might to such an extent that it posed a clear and present threat to Babylon. Persian armies under King Cyrus were advancing toward the city of Babylon, but for inexplicable reasons, Belshazzar chose to ignore this imminent threat in favor of a banquet for upward of a thousand royal guests. It was at this ill-conceived banquet that Daniel made his next prophetic appearance as the Babylonian Empire toppled before the emerging Persian Empire.

THE WRITING ON THE WALL

Belshazzar's opulent banquet led to the consumption of a great deal of wine, as well as to the concomitant intoxication that followed it. As the festivities unfolded, Belshazzar ordered his servants to fetch the gold and silver bowls that Nebuchadnezzar had previously plundered from the Temple in Jerusalem. He and his guests and concubines then drank from these bowls and offered praises to the gods of Babylon. It was at this point that the festive timbre of the banquet began to change.

> *Suddenly a human hand appeared and began writing on the plaster wall of the palace, where the light from the lamps was shining most brightly. And the king saw the hand as it was writing.*
>
> *He turned pale and was so frightened that his knees began to shake. He shouted for someone to bring in the magicians, wizards and astrologers...but none of them could read the writing or tell the king what it meant. In his distress King Belshazzar grew even paler and his noblemen had no idea what to do. (Daniel 5:5-9)*

At the insistence of the Queen Mother, Belshazzar then summoned Daniel to decipher the written words and ascertain their message. Daniel refused the gifts that Belshazzar offered to him, and conveyed their message:

> *You acted against the Lord of heaven and brought in the cups and bowls taken from His Temple.*

> *You, your noblemen, your wives, and your concubines drank wine out of them and praised gods made out of gold, silver, bronze, iron, wood and stone - gods that cannot see or hear and that do not know anything. But you did not honor the God Who determines whether you live or die and Who controls everything you do. That is why God has sent the hand to write these words.*
>
> *This is what was written: "[Mene, Mene, Tekel, Upharsin] Number, number, weight, divisions." And this is what it means: Number: God has numbered the days of your kingdom and brought it to an end; weight: you have been weighed on the scales and found to be too light; divisions: your kingdom is divided up and given to the Medes and the Persians. (Daniel 5:23-28)*

Before the night was over, Belshazzar had been killed and King Cyrus of Persia seized power - bringing the Babylonian Empire to its end. Daniel had again demonstrated his God-given ability of interpretation, and his administrative talents, devotion and wisdom would continue to find expression in the new Persian Empire.

THE PERSIAN CONQUEST OF BABYLON

It is rather remarkable that Persia's conquest of Babylon happened so abruptly and bloodlessly. While the leading political and social figures of Babylon reveled with Belshazzar, the forces of King Cyrus of Persia successfully diverted the flow of the Euphrates River into Babylon and entered the city without resistance via the now shallow and drying river bed of the original path of the Euphrates. It is believed that Belshazzar was killed at this time and his father Nabonidus captured upon his return to the city. The rule of the Persians had now begun.

The advent of Persian rule has resulted in a great deal of historical confusion due to a "clash of testimonies." The Book of Daniel refers to "Darius the Mede" as the first Persian overlord appointed by King Cyrus to rule Babylon, but the *Babylonian Chronicles* from the same time period list a different Mede - Gubaru (also known as Ugbaru or Gobryas) - as Cyrus' appointed overlord. The Book of Daniel also refers to the reigns of both "King Darius" and "King Cyrus," but there is some question as to whether Darius was ever given the title "King" by Cyrus after the conquest of Babylon. However, both the historical records of Babylon and the Book of Daniel agree on the method chosen by Darius (or Gubaru or Ugbaru or Gobryas) to administer the kingdom:

> *Darius decided to appoint 120 governors to hold office throughout his empire. In addition, he chose Daniel and two others to supervise the governors and to look after the king's interests.*
>
> *Daniel soon showed that he could do better work than the other supervisors or the governors.*
>
> *Because he was so outstanding, the king considered putting him in charge of the whole empire. (Daniel 6:1-3)*

It was this possible promotion of Daniel to the role of "prime minister" that inflamed the other administrators, who resented the idea of a Judean outranking them. They then began to plot against him, but the administrative prowess of Daniel, who was 82 years old at this time, was so impeccable, and his record so exemplary, that they were forced to abandon any possible plans to impugn his administrative service.

> *They said to each other, "We are not going to find anything of which to accuse Daniel unless it is something in connection with his religion." (Daniel 6:5)*

This set the stage for the most famous and most oft-repeated tale of the life of Daniel.

DANIEL IN THE LIONS' DEN

In his text *The Major Prophets* (1992), Dr. James E. Smith outlined the plot. "The officers devised a plan in which they would persuade the king to proclaim himself the sole representative of the deity for a period of thirty days. Since some Persian kings regarded themselves as deities, such a suggestion was not at all inconceivable. All petitions were to be addressed to him. Any person offering a religious petition to man or god during the thirty days would be executed in the lions' den. Such an edict would place Daniel in an awkward position. If he obeyed it, he would not be able to pray openly to his God. Yet if he disobeyed it, he would appear to be disloyal to the king whom he devoutly served. The suggestion appealed to the ego of the new king. He...did not hesitate to sign the document which his subordinates had prepared. Once he did, however, the edict became irrevocable."

Daniel was aware of the edict and its implications, and understood that it was aimed at undermining him. He was also aware that the king had been manipulated into signing such an edict which, under Persian law, was irreversible. Yet, Daniel was resolved not to alter or compromise his relationship with God.

When Daniel learned that the order had been signed, he went home. In an upstairs room of his house there were windows that faced toward Jerusalem. There, just as he had always done, he knelt down at the open windows and prayed to God three times a day. (Daniel 6:10)

This was, of course, what Daniel's rivals and detractors had been hoping to see. They immediately reported him to King Darius, reminded the king of the edict, and insisted that the edict be enforced. Outmaneuvered by his subordinates and stymied by the intractability of Persian law, a despondent Kind Darius was forced to accede to their wishes and place Daniel in the den of lions, but not before expressing to Daniel his hope that:

May your God, Whom you serve so loyally, rescue you. (Daniel 6:16)

After a fitful, sleepless night, the anxious king returned to the lions' den early the next morning and called out to Daniel. He was overjoyed when Daniel responded:

May Your Majesty live forever! God sent His angel to shut the mouths of the lions so that they would not hurt me. He did this because He knew that I was innocent and because I have not wronged you, Your Majesty. (Daniel 6:21-22)

After releasing Daniel from the pit, King Darius ordered that all of Daniel's accusers - along with their families - be thrown into the lions' den, where they were immediately attacked. Then King Darius issued the following proclamation:

> *Greetings! I command that throughout my empire everyone should fear and respect Daniel's God. He is a living God, and He will rule forever. His kingdom will never be destroyed, and His power will never come to an end. He saves and rescues; He performs wonders and miracles in heaven and on earth. He saved Daniel from being killed by the lions. (Daniel 6:25-28)*

The final prophetic experience of Daniel appropriately began with Daniel in the throes of deep and heartfelt prayer. Donned in sackcloth and sitting in ashes, Daniel admitted to Yahweh the multitude of sins committed by his people (including himself in their number) and praised the faithfulness, justice and mercy of God:

> *Lord God, You are great and we honor You. You are faithful to Your covenant and show constant love to those who love You and do what You command.*
>
> *We have sinned, we have done evil, we have done wrong. We have rejected what You commanded us to do and have turned away from what You showed us was right. We have not listened to Your servants, the prophets...You, Lord, always do what is right, but we have always brought disgrace on ourselves....You are merciful and forgiving, although we have rebelled against You...You did what You said You would do to us and our rulers. You punished Jerusalem more than any other city on earth, giving us all the punishment described in the Law of Moses. But even now, O Lord our God, we have not tried to please You by turning from our sins or by following Your truth. (Daniel 9:4-13)*

As Daniel continued to pray, his prayer changed from one of praise and contrition to one of petition for mercy and restitution:

> *"...Do not be angry with Jerusalem any longer. It is Your city, Your sacred hill...O God, hear my prayer and pleading. Restore Your Temple, which has been destroyed; restore it so that everyone will know that You are God...We are*

praying to You because You are merciful, not because we have done right. Lord, hear us. Lord, forgive us. Lord, listen to us and act! In order that everyone will know that You are God, do not delay! This city and these people are Yours. (Daniel 9:16-19)

GABRIEL'S EXPLANATION

It was at this point in Daniel's prayer that he encountered the angel Gabriel for the second time. Gabriel's arrival signaled that Daniel's prayer had been heard, and that Gabriel would explain to Daniel a prophecy that would address his prayers:

Daniel, I have come here to help you understand...When you began to plead with God, He answered you. He loves you, and so I have come to tell you the answer. Now pay attention...Seven times seventy years [490 years] is the length of time God has set for freeing your people and your holy city from sin and evil. Sin will be forgiven and eternal justice established ...and the holy Temple will be rededicated. Note this and understand it:

From the time the command is given to rebuild Jerusalem until God's chosen leader comes, seven times seven years [49 years] will pass. Jerusalem will be rebuilt...and will stand for seven times sixty-two years [434 years], but this will be a time of troubles. And at the end of that time God's chosen leader will be killed unjustly. The city and the Temple will be destroyed by the invading army of a powerful ruler. The end will come like a flood, bringing the war and destruction which God has prepared. (Daniel 9:22-27)

Many Biblical scholars look at these words of Gabriel and relate them directly to Jesus. The "time the command is given to rebuild Jerusalem" is interpreted as 457 BCE, when Ezra, the priest and scribe, began to rebuild Jerusalem, and the 483 years that follow (49 years to complete construction followed by 434 years for duration) led to the year 26 CE - when Jesus was baptized in the River Jordan and began His public ministry, only to "be killed unjustly" in 30 CE before the "city and the Temple were destroyed by the invading army of a powerful ruler" - the Roman-initiated Diaspora of 70 CE.

This prayer of Daniel and Gabriel's response to it - which gave Daniel a sweeping panoramic view of salvation history over the next half-millenium - is an incredible tribute to a man whose devotion and fidelity to his God and people never wavered throughout his life.

HERO PROPHET - OR FICTIONAL SYMBOL?

The story of Daniel's life is one of the most inspirational sagas in the Old Testament. A young boy is forcibly removed from his family and homeland and brought to a distant, foreign country by the soldiers of his conqueror. While in captivity, even though treated civilly, he is forced to learn the language, literature and customs of his oppressors, who actively seek to indoctrinate him into a new lifestyle with new loyalties and values. Even his name is changed to reflect his separation from his previous life and identity. Yet he refuses to yield to the high-powered pressures placed upon him and remains faithful to his own God and people. How can anyone read this story and fail to marvel at Daniel's dedication, faith and commitment to God and country in the face of such intense proselytization? The big question is: is it all a lie?

Increasingly, Biblical scholars are doubting the existence of Daniel as an authentic, historically-verified 6th century BCE prophet and hero. In analyzing the writing style and vocabulary of the Book of Daniel, several historical inaccuracies or inconsistencies, as well as the specificity of details found in both his own visions as well as in the dreams of others that he interpreted, they are coming to believe that, in all likelihood, the book ascribed to Daniel was written much, much later - most probably in the mid-2nd century BCE to inspire a Judean population ruled and oppressed by Greek overlords. One of these overlords, King Antiochus IV Epiphanes, attempted to forcibly compel the people of Judah to pay homage to the gods and goddesses of Greece. He went so far as to desecrate the Temple of Jerusalem by filling it with idols of the Greek deities and demanding proper adoration of these gods under threat of severe punishment. It was this coercion that led to the Maccabean Revolt and the ouster of the Greeks from Judah in 142 BCE. It is thought that the author of the Book of Daniel, not wanting to further inflame Antiochus by "calling him out" by name, tried to inspire his fellow Judeans not to yield to this pressure by pointing to other Judeans (Daniel and his three friends) who faced - and overcame - similar pressures to reject Yahweh at an earlier time in Judean history.

The jury is out. Some theologians remain convinced that Daniel was an authentic prophet, hero and role model at the time of the Babylonian and Persian Empires, while others see him as nothing more than a fictional symbol of resistance. The ultimate answer to this question remains shrouded in the mists of history, but it would be shallow and incomplete not to acknowledge this ongoing enigma.

UNIQUE LITERATURE: TRILINGUAL, BI-PERSONAL, APOCALYPTIC

And lastly, a final note (or two) must be included about the Book of Daniel itself. While this text hopes to focus its primary attention on the lives and ministries of the prophets themselves, the unique composition of the Book of Daniel merits special consideration.

Daniel is one of the Old Testament books that is composed in multiple languages - Hebrew and Aramaic - but also contains additions written in Greek. For the most part, the sections of Daniel that deal specifically with issues of Judaism and the Judean people are written in Hebrew, while those sections that address the rise and fall of other empires are composed in Aramaic, which was the dominant language of the Middle Eastern world at that time. Certainly the rationale for this dichotomy can be easily explained, and a 6th century BCE Daniel would undoubtedly be fluent in both languages, but it might also be inferred that the book could be the product of several authors, rather than one, and that multiple authors might be composing their contributions at different moments in history. Catholic Old Testaments also contain additional material that was written in Greek - material not viewed as authentically canonical by many Protestant denominations, who place it in a separate section of the Bible called the *Apocrypha*, or "secret" writings. This additional material embellishes the story of Shadrach, Meshach and Abednego in the fiery furnace as well as offers several other stories about Daniel's wisdom - the tales of "Susanna" and her efforts to clear her good name from a blackmail scandal, and the stories of "Bel and the Dragon," where Daniel demonstrates the falsity of two of the gods of Babylon. In Catholic translations of the Book of Daniel, the story of Shadrach, Meshach and Abednego is included in chapter 3 between verses 23 and 24. The story of Susanna is added as chapter 13, and the stories of Bel and the Dragon become chapter 14.

The events in the Book of Daniel are not arranged in chronological order, so there is great difficulty in relating the events in Daniel's life in sequential order. Daniel is divided into two main sections: chapters 1-6 address the events in the lives of Daniel and his three friends as they endeavored to remain faithful to their God within the Babylonian and Persian Empires, and chapters 7-12 relate the prophetic dreams and visions of Daniel as well as their possible interpretation. Interestingly, chapters 1-6 are written in the third person, while chapters 7-12 are composed in the first person - which might also suggest that they were written by different authors.

It must be mentioned also, as one final note about the uniqueness of the Book of Daniel, that it is the pre-eminent Old Testament example of a style of writing known as *apocalyptic literature*. "Apocalyptic" is derived from a Greek word for "revelation" and purports to unveil previously hidden truths. These revelations are often eschatological prophecies of the "end times," contain many convoluted symbols and images, and are often presented through the medium of divine or celestial messengers. Chapters 7-12 in the Book of Daniel are clear examples of this style of writing, as they offer visions of the future through dramatic physical symbols and actions, whose meanings are explained through the ministrations of angels such as Gabriel.

The Book of Daniel contains more examples of apocalyptic writing than any other books of the Old Testament, and this may be due to the possible Persian influences on the author of Daniel, if indeed the Book was composed in the 6th century BCE. The Persian Empire, serving an an historical backdrop to Daniel, embraced Zoroastrianism as its state religion - a dualistic faith that placed great emphasis on the contrasts between good and evil, light and darkness and angels and demons, and employed other dramatic symbols portraying the consequences of moral and immoral behavior.

Several other examples of apocalyptic writing can be found in the Books of the prophets Isaiah, Jeremiah, Ezekiel, Zechariah and Joel, and the Book of Revelation is the pre-eminent example of apocalyptic literature in the New Testament.

CHAPTER 12: QUESTIONS FOR REVIEW

1. Why was Daniel brought to Babylon by the forces of King Nebuchadnezzar?
2. How were Daniel and his friends treated in the court of Babylon?
3. What were the details of the first nightmare that troubled Nebuchadnezzar?
4. Why were Nebuchadnezzar's advisors unable to offer an interpretation of his dream?
5. What was Daniel's explanation of the symbols in Nebuchadnezzar's dream?
6. Why were Shadrach, Meshach and Abednego thrown into the fiery furnace - and what happened to them in the furnace?
7. Why did Daniel hesitate to interpret Nebuchadnezzar's second dream?
8. What is *zoanthropy* and why was Nebuchadnezzar afflicted with it?
9. What role did Daniel play in the administration of the Babylonian Empire?
10. When the Persians defeated the Babylonians, what happened to Daniel?

11. What is the connection between Nebuchadnezzar's first dream and Daniel's dream of the Four Beasts?
12. What did the Four Beasts represent?
13. What was foreshadowed by Daniel's vision of the Ram and the Goat?
14. What is meant by the cryptic words "Mene, Mene, Tekel, Upharsin?"
15. What plot against Daniel led to him being thrown into a den of lions?
16. What are the characteristics of *apocalyptic* literature?
17. In what other ways is the Book of Daniel unique in the way it is written?

Chapter Thirteen
JONAH

"I am better off dead than alive"

When many people contemplate or discuss the Hebrew Scriptures, I doubt that they describe these sacred writings with adjectives such as progressive, broad-minded, permissive or liberal. Perhaps their descriptions would lead them to the opposite conclusion - that the Scriptures reflect a traditional, conservative mindset permeated with the faint scent of mold or rancidity. Yet can't a case for libertarianism be made for a volume that places "center stage" a hand-picked messenger of God who essentially thumbs his nose at God and refuses to complete his divine assignment? Can't we see a streak of broad-mindedness in a book that immortalizes one who *eventually* (after a rather dramatic learning experience and exercise in humility) delivers God's message - only to reject and disparage that same message? In so many ways, Jonah is much less a prophet, and so much more an "anti-prophet."

It should be noted up front that Jonah is recognized by many Biblical scholars as a fictional character. At least the *events* in his life have been fictionalized insofar as there is an actual burial site for Jonah - recently destroyed by the forces of ISIS - in Mosul, Iraq.

Jonah was a prophet who is thought to have lived in the northern kingdom of Israel in the 8th century BCE. The Hebrew Scriptures provide scant information about his personal life, other than the fact that he was the son of Amittai. When his story begins, God instructs Jonah:

> *"Go to Nineveh, that great city, and speak out against it; I am aware of how wicked its people are." (Jonah 1:2)*

Nineveh was the capital city of Assyria, a powerful civilization to the northeast, that Israel viewed as an enemy state due to its ongoing program of conquest and expansion. While the Bible does not explicitly state Jonah's reasons for his actions, the presumption is that Jonah resented God for reaching out to the sworn enemies of Israel. He questioned why God would offer a chance at redemption to a society that opposed and threatened Israel, God's own Chosen People. So Jonah took matters into his own hands and chose the path of direct disobedience to God:

> *Jonah...set out in the opposite direction in order to get away from the Lord. He went to Joppa, where he found a ship about to go to Spain. He paid his fare and went aboard with the crew to sail to Spain... (Jonah 1:3)*

There is no evidence that Jonah spoke with God either to ask Him to explain His actions or to try to dissuade God from assigning him to such an unsavory task. He simply "took off" - motivations unclear.

There may be several morals to the story of Jonah. If one of them is that it is not possible to hide from the Lord - that God knows all and sees all - then that message resounded loudly and clearly through the dramatic events that followed:

> *...the Lord sent a strong wind on the sea, and the storm was so violent that the ship was in danger of breaking up. The sailors were terrified and cried out for help, each one to his own god...Meanwhile...Jonah was lying in the ship's hold, sound asleep. (Jonah 1:4-5)*

As the storm grew worse, the sailors inexplicably decided to draw lots to determine who should be blamed for the crisis enveloping them. When Jonah's name was drawn, he admitted that he was an Israelite who was running away from his God. The storm's intensity increased, and Jonah offered the sailors a possible escape:

> *Throw me into the sea, and it will calm down. I know it is my fault that you are caught in this violent storm. (Jonah 1:12)*

The sailors respected Jonah's confession to such an extent that they wanted to use that option only as a last resort. They valiantly tried to row the ship to calmer waters near the shoreline, but to no avail. Eventually, after exhausting all other options, they were forced to implement Jonah's suggestion.

> *Then they picked Jonah up and threw him into the sea, and it calmed down at once...At the Lord's command, a large fish swallowed Jonah, and he was inside the fish for three days and three nights. (Jonah 1:15-17)*

Comparisons are often made between Jonah's three days in the belly of the fish and the three days that Jesus spent in the tomb. While incarcerated in the fish, Jonah had ample time to review the decisions he made that led him to the predicament in which he found himself. His change in attitude was reflected in his prayer from inside his cetacean cell:

> *In my distress, O Lord, I called to You, and You answered me. From deep in the world of the dead I cried for help, and You heard me. You threw me down into the depths, to the very bottom of the sea, where the waters were all around me, and all Your mighty waves rolled over me. I thought I had been banished from Your presence and would never see Your holy Temple again. The water came over me and choked me; the sea covered me completely, and seaweed wrapped around my head. I went down to the very roots of the mountains, into the land whose gates lock shut forever. But You, O Lord my God, brought me back from the depths alive. When I felt my life slipping away, then, O Lord, I prayed to You, and in Your holy Temple You heard me. Those who worship worthless idols have abandoned their loyalty to You. But I will sing praises to You; I will offer You a sacrifice and do what I have promised. Salvation comes from the Lord! (Jonah 2:2-9)*

The Lord instructed the fish to spit Jonah onto the beach, and Jonah was given a second chance to complete his ministerial assignment. This time, Jonah headed straight for Nineveh and proclaimed to its citizens:

> *In forty days Nineveh will be destroyed. (Jonah 3:4)*

It is rather remarkable that the people of Nineveh - from the king to the common folk - heard the message of this foreigner (and possible enemy) and took it to heart.

The people of Nineveh believed God's message. So they decided that everyone should fast, and all the people, from the greatest to the least, put on sackcloth to show that they had repented.

> *When the king of Nineveh heard about it, he got up from his throne, took off his robe, put on sackcloth and sat down in ashes. He sent out a proclamation to the people of Nineveh: "…No one is to eat anything; all persons, cattle and sheep are forbidden to eat or drink. All persons and animals must wear sackcloth. Everyone must pray earnestly to God and must give up his wicked behavior and his evil actions. Perhaps God will change His mind; perhaps He will stop being angry, and we will not die!" (Jonah 3:5-9)*

It would make perfect sense at this point for Jonah to be quite pleased with himself. He had completed his mission, and its success was monumental. His Assyrian enemies, who did not even worship Yahweh, had heart Jonah's message and responded to it with great faith and contrition. Wicked people had turned from their evil ways and embraced the path of righteousness. But Jonah not only was not satisfied - he was resentful of the Lord's actions.

> *Lord, didn't I say before I left home that this is just what You would do? That's why I did my best to run away to Spain! I knew that You are a loving and merciful God, always patient, always kind, and always ready to change Your mind and not punish. Now then, Lord, let me die. I am better off dead than alive. (Jonah 4:2-3)*

So Jonah threw the equivalent of an adult tantrum because God relented from His threat of destruction when He saw the contrition of the Ninevites. And the Lord's response to Jonah's histrionics took the form of a question:

> *What right do you have to be angry? (Jonah 4:4)*

Clearly, a question with no good answer.

Jonah then departed Nineveh and camped to the east of the city, opting to remain nearby to see what would transpire. Perhaps he was hoping that the Lord would reverse Himself and punish the people of Nineveh after all. Hope springs eternal…

While Jonah waited in the heat of the day to observe the fate of Nineveh, he received a welcome surprise with an unwelcome ending:

> *Then the Lord made a plant grow up over Jonah to give him some shade, so that he would be more comfortable. Jonah was extremely pleased with the plant. But at dawn the next day, at God's command, a worm attacked the plant, and it died. After the sun has risen, God sent a hot east wind, and Jonah was about to faint from the heat of the sun beating down on his head. (Jonah 4:6-8)*

This led to the repeat of an earlier dialogue between Jonah and the Lord. Jonah said:

> *I am better off dead than alive…But God said to him, "What right do you have to be angry about the plant?" (Jonah 4:8-9)*

When Jonah replied that he had every right to be angry, God's response to Jonah underscored how petty and petulant Jonah had become:

> *The Lord said, "This plant grew up in one night and disappeared the next; you didn't do anything for it and you didn't make it grow - yet you feel sorry for it! How much more, then, should I have pity on Nineveh, that great city. After all, it has more than 120,000 innocent children in it, as well as many animals." (Jonah 4:10)*

The story of Jonah offers a number of important messages as well as presents several startling contrasts. It portrays God as the loving and compassionate Lord of all peoples - not just the Israelites - Who offers forgiveness and restitution to all who seek it, without "playing favorites." It also presents a God Who calls individuals into His service even if they are flawed themselves. And Jonah's selfishness, lack of compassion, immaturity and disobedience all demonstrate some rather serious character flaws.

The story also contrasts the Israelite belief that only the Chosen People are worthy of God's beneficence with the Lord's compassion even to the enemies of Israel, and it similarly contrasts the narrow-mindedness of Jonah with the panoramic vision of the Lord. Finally, how ironic is it that Jonah's very tepid pronouncement to the Ninevites was met with fervent acts of contrition and remorse while the impassioned pleas of other prophets to the people of Israel fell largely on deaf ears! The Book of Jonah offers much to think about in its four short chapters.

CHAPTER 13: QUESTIONS FOR REVIEW

1. Why is Jonah referred to as an "anti-prophet?"
2. What was unique about Jonah's call to preach to the people of Nineveh?
3. What happened to Jonah when he travelled in the opposite direction from the place God sent him to deliver His message?
4. What prompted Jonah to change his mind and deliver God's message to the Ninevites?
5. How did the Ninevites respond to Jonah's pronouncement?
6. What was Jonah's response to the Ninevites' reactions to his message?
7. What was the point of the" rise and fall' of the plant that offered shade to Jonah?
8. What are three important messages that come out of the story of Jonah?

ADDITIONAL PROPHETS OF NOTE

Chapter Fourteen

THE REMAINING "MINOR" PROPHETS

What we today call the "Old Testament" is similar - but not quite identical - to the original Hebrew Scriptures, or *Tanakh*. When the Christian Bible was first organized, the Church took it upon itself to re-name, re-structure and "re-stock" the Hebrew Scriptures. The Church opted to take the Tanakh, which consisted of 24 books (written in Hebrew with a touch of Aramaic), and re-organize it into 46 books (while also adding additional material written in Greek), re-brand it as the "Old Testament", and include a new corpus of literature (written exclusively in Greek) about the ministry of Jesus and the emergence of the early Church, which it christened (pun intended!) the "New Testament."

This metamorphosis is well-known to students of the Bible, but it may not be equally well-known that the Tanakh included a book simply entitled "The Twelve." This single volume contained the collected writings of twelve different prophets who lived and ministered between the ninth and fifth centuries BCE: Hosea, Joel, Amos, Obadiah, Jonah, Micah, Nahum, Habakkuk, Zephaniah, Haggai, Zechariah and Malachi. Inappropriately, these twelve became known as the Minor Prophets to separate their works from those of the Major Prophets - Isaiah, Jeremiah and Ezekiel. The designations "Major" and "Minor" are incredibly misleading, suggesting - as discussed in Chapter 1 - that the words of Isaiah, Jeremiah and Ezekiel were more important than those of The Twelve. Rather, the designations refer only to the length of the respective writings of these prophet-authors - the Books of the three Majors are simply much longer than those of the Twelve - but the content of each prophet's book is equally worthy of perusal and reflection.

This text purports to offer a survey of the lives and ministries of the Old Testament prophets in the hope that readers will be inspired to probe more deeply into their messages. For various reasons this text has already separated and highlighted the lives of four of these Twelve - Amos, Hosea, Jonah and Micah - but it would be short-sighted and incomplete to ignore the ministries of the other eight, so the following chapters will, albeit briefly, address the "remnant" of the Twelve. It should also be noted parenthetically that there are other prophets (and/or schools of prophets) mentioned by name throughout the Old Testament, yet virtually nothing of substance is recorded about their lives and ministries, so this text is grudgingly omitting them until, at some point in the future, perhaps forthcoming archaeological discoveries will shed new light upon them.

CHAPTER 14: QUESTIONS FOR REVIEW

1. What changes were made by the Church to the Hebrew Scriptures when the Christian Bible was in formation?
2. Which prophets' writings were included in the Tanakh's Book of "The Twelve?"
3. What is the difference between "Major" and "Minor" Prophets?

Chapter Fifteen
JOEL

"I will pour out My spirit on everyone"

In his book *The Message of the Prophets* (2010), J. Daniel Hays outlined the most perplexing problem faced by scholars and readers who opt to explore the Book of Joel when he pointed out that there is no other reference to Joel outside of this book, nor does it contain any other specific information that would indicate its proper time period in Judean history.

Hays went on to explain that Biblical scholars differ on their views of Joel's timeline, some suggesting that he lived as early as the ninth century BCE or as late as the fifth century BCE. That's 400 years of uncertainty!

The Book of Joel is only three chapters in length. After introducing Joel as the son of Pethuel, the book describes in great detail how a horrific invasion of locusts has decimated the land and deprived the people and livestock alike of the grain and fruits they needed to survive.

> *Grieve, you farmers; cry, you that take care of the vineyards, because the wheat, the barley, yes all the crops are destroyed. The grapevines and fig trees have withered; all the fruit trees have withered and died. (Joel 1:11-12)*

Joel interpreted this pestilence as a foreshadowing that a reckoning day will be forthcoming from God:

> *Blow the trumpet; sound the alarm on Zion, God's sacred hill. Tremble, people of Judah!*
>
> *The day of the Lord is coming soon. It will be a dark and gloomy day, a black and cloudy day.*
>
> *The great army of locusts advances like darkness spreading over the mountains. There has never been anything like it, and there never will be*

again...The Lord thunders commands to His army. The troops that obey Him are many and mighty. How terrible is the day of the Lord!

Who will survive it? (Joel 2:1-2,11)

Like so many of the other prophets, Joel believed that God could and would rescind His punishment if He saw a change of heart in the actions of His people. Without listing for the people of Judah a litany of their failings - probably assuming that they already knew where their shortcomings lie - Joel outlined the next steps they should take:

Repent sincerely and return to [the Lord] with fasting and weeping and mourning. Let your broken heart show your sorrow; tearing your clothes is not enough. Come back to the Lord your God. He is kind and full of mercy; He is patient and keeps His promise; He is always ready to forgive and not punish. Perhaps the Lord your God will change His mind and bless you with abundant crops. Then you can offer Him grain and wine. (Joel 2:12-14)

Joel went on to paint a picture of the mercy of God Who only wants the best for His people and showers them not only with the necessities they require for survival - but with His Spirit as well:

Then the Lord showed concern for His land; He had mercy on His people... "Now I am going to give you grain and wine and olive oil, and you will be satisfied. Other nations will no longer despise you. I will remove the locust army that came from the north...I will destroy them because of all they have done to you...Animals, don't be afraid. The pastures are green; the trees bear their fruit, and there are plenty of figs and grapes...The threshing places will be full of grain...I will give you back what you lost...Then, Israel, you will know that I am among you and that I, the Lord, am your God and there is no other...Afterward I will pour out My Spirit on everyone...At that time I will pour out My Spirit even on servants, both men and women." (Joel 2:18-29)

The final words of Joel addressed a future day of judgment when God will judge all of the enemies and conquerors of Israel who have scattered the Chosen People, enslaved them, plundered their land and their homes, and stolen the treasures of the Temple. In the "Valley of Judgment," God will

> ...*cut them down like grain at harvest time [and] crush them as grapes are crushed in a full wine press until the wine runs over. (Joel 3:13)*

CHAPTER 15: QUESTIONS FOR REVIEW

1. When did Joel serve as God's prophet?
2. What is the invasion of locusts meant to foreshadow in Joel's writing?
3. What suggestions did Joel make for the people to show God that they had mended their ways?

Chapter Sixteen
OBADIAH

"What you have done will be done to you"

The words of Obadiah are even more concise and focused that the previous words of Joel, and perhaps even less is known of Obadiah's life, except that his name means "servant of the Lord." His book addresses only one issue - the Edomites' delight at the Babylonian conquest of Judea in 586 BCE - so the presumption is made that Obadiah's words were recorded shortly after that historical occurrence near the beginning of the sixth century BCE.

One of the values that Obadiah emphasized was the importance of family loyalty. The Edomites were descendants of Esau, the brother of Jacob, whose descendants were, of course, the children of Israel. As you may recall, God changed Jacob's name to Israel over a thousand years earlier. Therefore, the Judeans and Edomites were related, even though they had grown apart and often clashed. When the Babylonians invaded Judah in 586 BCE, the Edomites gloated at the catastrophe that had befallen the Judeans. Not only did they gloat, but as Judeans fled the carnage and tried to escape to Edom in the south, the Edomites captured them and turned them over to the Babylonians. And if that wasn't bad enough, the Edomites then invaded Judea after the Babylonians left and scavenged whatever plunder was left behind.

Obadiah called the Edomites to task for their treachery:

> *Because you robbed and killed your brothers, the descendants of Jacob, you will be destroyed and dishonored forever. You stood aside on that day when enemies broke down their gates.*
>
> *You were as bad as those strangers who carried off Jerusalem's wealth and divided it among themselves. You should not have gloated over the misfortune of your brothers in Judah...You should not have laughed at them in their distress. You should not have entered the city of My people...to seize their riches on the day of their disaster. You should not have stood at the crossroads to catch those trying to escape. You should not have handed them over to the enemy... (Obadiah 1:10-14)*

But a mere reprimand for displaying such a lack of family loyalty - as well as avarice - was insufficient.

Obadiah also predicted future retribution when he conveyed the words of the Lord:

> *The day is near when I, the Lord, will judge all nations. Edom, what you have done will be done to you. You will get back what you have given...The people of Jacob and of Joseph will be like fire; they will destroy the people of Esau as fire burns stubble. No descendant of Esau will survive. I, the Lord, have spoken. (Obadiah 1:15,18)*

About 600 years later, St. Paul expressed the same sentiment in his epistle to the Galatians, when he wrote:

> *As you sow, so shall you reap. (Galatians 6:7)*

In today's jargon we'd be more likely to say something like, "Whatever goes around, comes around." All variations of the same theme.

CHAPTER 16: QUESTIONS FOR REVIEW

1. Who were the Edomites, and why did Obadiah condemn them?
2. What prediction was made by Obadiah about the future of the Edomites?

Chapter Seventeen
NAHUM

"I will... break the chains that bind you"

The story of Jonah in the eighth century BCE related the psychological conflict faced by a prophet who was tasked by God to offer a message of forgiveness to a people he felt were unworthy to receive it. Yet, ultimately, he delivered God's message to a violent people - the Ninevites - who turned away from their sins and sought God's mercy. Well, apparently that conversion was short-lived, because the mid-seventh century BCE prophecy of Nahum is directed exclusively against those same Ninevites upon their prompt return to their evil, violent ways.

Nineveh was the capital of the Assyrian Empire, an incredibly violent and repressive culture that relished the use of torture and atrocity of all shapes and sizes. The Assyrians, for example, would impale the corpses of their victims on spikes for use as decorations, in much the same way as the Romans used crucifixions. They would grab babies by their ankles and smash them against stone walls and pavements. They flayed the skins of their enemies and hung them on walls as works of art. Their depravities were beyond horrific. When Nahum predicted in the mid-seventh century BCE that Nineveh would fall, his prophecy was the result of a vision he had experienced. Except for this recorded vision, and the fact that Nahum hailed from the village of Elkosh (which no historian or cartographer has yet been able to locate), nothing else is know of his life. Like the prophet Joel, all we know of Nahum is what is written in the Old Testament book ascribed to him.

The Book of Nahum is a reminder to the Chosen People that evil will always be vanquished - it will never endure. The point of Nahum's writing was to reassure the people of Judah that Assyria's reign of terror was about to end. It was written for the benefit of the Judeans, even though its message was directed to the Ninevites. Several random excerpts will suffice to convey its simple and direct message:

> *The Lord is good; He protects His people in times of trouble; He takes care of those who turn to Him. Like a great rushing flood He completely destroys His enemies; He sends to their death those who oppose Him."* (Nahum 1:7-8)

This is what the Lord says to His people Israel: "Even though the Assyrians are strong and numerous, they will be destroyed and disappear...I will now end Assyria's power over you and break the chains that bind you." (Nahum 1:12-13)

This is what the Lord has decreed about the Assyrians: "They will have no descendants to carry on their name. I will destroy the idols that are in the temples of their gods. I am preparing a grave for the Assyrians - they don't deserve to live." (Nahum 1:14)

The Lord Almighty says, "I will punish you, Nineveh! I will strip you naked and let the nations see you, see you in all your shame. I will treat you with contempt and cover you with filth. People will stare at you in horror." (Nahum 2:5-6)

CHAPTER 17: QUESTIONS FOR REVIEW

1. What was so disturbing about the violent behavior of the Ninevites?
2. Why did Nahum write this book?
3. What prediction did Nahum make about the final destiny of the Assyrians?

Chapter Eighteen
HABAKKUK

"O Lord, how long must I cry for help before You listen?"

As with Joel and Nahum, Habakkuk was yet another prophet about whom very little was known. It seems that these shorter books of the Old Testament are as short as they are because - among other things - they failed to include any biographical information about their authors. However, in the case of Habakkuk, the Lord's words to him:

> I am bringing the Babylonians to power, those fierce, restless people. (Habakkuk 1:6)

suggested that Habakkuk very possibly lived and ministered in the days immediately prior to the Babylonian invasion of Judah in 586 BCE. This would make Habakkuk a contemporary of both Jeremiah and Ezekiel.

Habakkuk's opening words began a dialogue with God, but Habakkuk's tone bordered on either insolence, impatience or despair:

> O Lord, how long must I call for help before You listen, before You save us from violence? Why do You make me see such trouble? How can You stand to look on such wrongdoing? Destruction and violence are all around me, and there is fighting and quarreling everywhere. The law is weak and useless, and justice is never done. Evil men get the better of the righteous, and so justice is perverted. (Habakkuk 1:2-4)

Was Habakkuk complaining to God that He was failing His own people, or was he just frustrated that the times were hard? His words read like a chastisement of the Lord, but they did begin a dialogue with God Whose reply was not the response that Habakkuk was hoping to hear. The Lord said:

I am going to do something that you will not believe when you hear about it. I am bringing the Babylonians to power, those fierce, restless people. They are marching out across the world to conquer other lands. They spread fear and terror..." (Habakkuk 1:5-7)

Habakkuk couldn't believe his ears. He complained to God about the prevalence of violence and injustice, and God's response was to announce that even more violence and injustice would be forthcoming, delivered at the hands of a civilization known for its abject brutality. What's wrong with this picture? Clearly this was not the answer Habakkuk was expecting to hear. So Habakkuk issued yet another complaint, perhaps more virulent that his previous one:

Lord...You are My God, holy and eternal...But how can You stand these treacherous, evil men?...So why are You silent while they destroy people who are more righteous than they are? How can You treat people like fish or like a swarm of insects?... (Habakkuk 1:12-14)

So God responded to Habakkuk yet again:

Write down clearly on tablets what I reveal to you, so that it can be read at a glance....It is not yet time for it to come true. But the time is coming quickly...And this is the message: Those who are evil will not survive, but those who are righteous will live because they are faithful to God. (Habakkuk 2:2-4)

At this point, Habakkuk acquiesced - and saw the value in trusting God to have devised a plan that would insure ultimate justice and righteousness. Chapter 3 of Habakkuk - very different from the prose of the first two chapters - expresses in the form of a psalm how Habakkuk had "come around." He sang:

I will quietly wait for the time to come when God will punish those who attack us. (Habakkuk 3:16)

CHAPTER 18: QUESTIONS FOR REVIEW

1. During what time period did Habakkuk (apparently) live?
2. Why did Habakkuk seem frustrated with the Lord?
3. What pronouncement of the Lord did Habakkuk find incredulous?
4. Why is Chapter 3 of the Book of Habakkuk different in tone from the first two chapters?

Chapter Nineteen
ZEPHANIAH

"I am going to destroy everything on earth..."

Canto III of Dante's *Inferno* opens with an inscription above the portal to Hell which expresses one of the most frightening sentiments ever put to paper: "Abandon hope, all you who enter here." In other words, when one passed through that opening into Hell, one was perpetually, eternally doomed - beyond even the virtue of hope. Wow! Powerful stuff! But the opening words of Zephaniah do not play "sloppy seconds" to Dante. They are equally terrifying and completely uncompromising:

> *The Lord said, "I am going to destroy everything on earth, all human beings and animals, birds and fish. I will bring about the downfall of the wicked. I will destroy all mankind, and no survivors will be left. I, the Lord, have spoken." (Zephaniah 1:2-3)*

The prophet Zephaniah is believed to have been of royal blood, a descendant of the righteous King Hezekiah, who ruled Judah from 715 - 686 BCE. The brief genealogy of Zephaniah that opens his book suggests that his ministry took place during the reign of King Josiah, before his spiritual reform initiatives of 621 BCE. It was during this time period that faith in God and conformity to the requirements of the Covenant were in very short supply. In his 1998 handbook *Get Into the Bible: Journey Through the Greatest Story of All Time*, Steven M. Miller pointed out that "Zephaniah lived in a day when most Jews didn't worship God any longer. They worshipped gods of other nations, and even sacrificed their children to appease the idols. They cheated each other to accumulate wealth for themselves. They showed nothing but disdain for the people whom God repeatedly told them to take care of: the poor, the widows, the orphans."

Is it any wonder then that the words of Zephaniah were so harsh and unyielding? Clearly the Lord had ample reason - given the profundity of His people's violations of the Covenant - to voice sentiments of such fury and utter disappointment. The threat that opened the Book of Zephaniah was just the "tip of the iceberg" in conveying the wrath of God. Zephaniah continued to convey God's anger:

I will punish the people of Jerusalem and of all Judah. I will destroy the last trace of the worship of Baal there, and no one will even remember the pagan priests who serve him.

I will destroy anyone who goes up on the roof and worships the sun, the moon, and the stars. I will also destroy those who worship Me and swear loyalty to Me, but then takes oaths in the name of the god Molech. (Zephaniah 1:4-5)

Like so many prophets before him, Zechariah then turned from these dire threats to implore the Chosen People to change their ways:

Shameless nation, come to your senses before you are driven away like chaff blown by the wind, before the burning anger of the Lord comes upon you, before the day when He shows His fury. Turn to the Lord, all you humble people of the land who obey His commands. Do what is right and humble yourselves before the Lord. Perhaps you will escape punishment on the day when the Lord shows His anger. (Zephaniah 2:1-3)

Zephaniah also made it clear that the retribution of the Lord would not be directed solely against the people of Judah. Rather, other nations who are guilty of grievous sin would likewise be vanquished:

No one will be left in the city of Gaza. Ashkelon will be deserted. The people of Ashdod will be driven out in half a day, and the people of Ekron will be driven from their city. You Philistines are doomed...The Lord has passed sentence on you...Moab and Ammon are going to be destroyed like Sodom and Gomorrah...The Lord will also put the people of Ethiopia to death. The Lord will use His power to destroy Assyria. He will make the city of Nineveh a deserted ruin, a waterless desert. (Zephaniah 2:4-13)

Certainly, Zephaniah has foretold of a future that offers nothing but destruction and anguish not only to the people of Judah, but also to any of the surrounding tribes and cultures who have proven themselves to be evil and undeserving of salvation. The cities mentioned above were prominent metropolitan areas in modern day Jordan and Iraq, so God's threats extended beyond Jerusalem and Judah. As cataclysmic as Zephaniah's pronouncements were, his ministry ended on a more positive note with the promise that God would collect His faithful survivors and reward them with an end to sorrow, injustice and violence:

> *Sing and shout for joy, people of Israel!... The Lord has stopped your punishment; He has removed all your enemies...there is no reason now to be afraid...The Lord will take delight in you, and in His love He will give you new life. He will...make you prosperous once again. (Zephaniah 3:14-20)*

CHAPTER 19: QUESTIONS FOR REVIEW

1. What is so frightening about the opening words in the Book of Zephaniah?
2. What background information is available about the life of Zephaniah?
3. How did the people of Judah earn the wrath of God through their behavior?
4. Which other peoples beside the Judeans were also threatened by Zephaniah?

Chapter Twenty
HAGGAI

"Why should you be living in well-built houses while My Temple lies in ruins?"

Haggai's ministry to the people of Judah began close to a century after that of Zephaniah. Biblical historians estimate Haggai's message at about 520 BCE. By this time, the Persians had conquered the Babylonians and permitted the Judeans who had been carried off to Babylon to return home. Under Zerubbabel, their governor, and Joshua, their High Priest, thousands of Judeans returned to Judah to rebuild their homes and their lives. But it was through the words of Haggai that the Judeans came to realize that, in the eyes of Yahweh, they had been "putting the cart before the horse." Through Haggai the Lord said:

> *My people, why should you be living in well-built houses while My Temple lies in ruins?...Now go up into the hills, get lumber, and rebuild the Temple; then I will be pleased and will be worshipped as I should be. (Haggai 1:4,8)*

The returnees from Babylon had previously begun to lay the foundation for a new Temple 18 years earlier, but had abandoned their efforts when some local opposition challenged them, and shifted their energies to their own personal concerns. It was time for their focus to shift back to their "unfinished business" and re-order their priorities. The Lord also made it clear that He was preventing the people from achieving greater prosperity because of the disrespect they had shown Him by failing to rebuild His house.

The new Temple lacked the opulence and majesty of its predecessor because the people lacked the resources and wealth of King Solomon. However, the Lord was more concerned with the efforts and dedication of the people in honoring Him - not on the amount of gold and silver they were able to add as embellishments:

> *Is there anyone among you who can still remember how splendid the Temple used to be? How does it look to you now? It must seem like nothing at all. But now don't be discouraged, any of you. Do the work, for I am with you...All the silver and gold of the world is Mine. The new Temple will be more splendid than the old one, and there I will give My people prosperity and peace. The Lord Almighty has spoken. (Haggai 1:3-9)*

CHAPTER 20: QUESTIONS FOR REVIEW

1. Where and when did Haggai live and prophesize?
2. In what way did Haggai suggest that the people show the Lord their dedication to Him?

Chapter Twenty-One
ZECHARIAH

"Your king is coming to you...humble and riding on a donkey"

Zechariah is a perfect example of why the term "Minor Prophets" is misleading and inappropriate, because the 14 chapters of the book ascribed to him are replete with insight and vision - there's nothing "minor" about them either in terms of content or length. Fortunately, unlike some of the other prophets, we do know something of Zechariah's background; he was a priest who was born while in captivity in Babylon, the son of Berechiah and the grandson of Iddo, both of whom were also priests. We are also aware of the dates of Zechariah's ministry - 520-518 BCE - from Zechariah's own hand:

> *In the eighth month of the second year that Darius was emperor of Persia, the Lord gave this message... (Zechariah 1:1)*

It should be remembered that after the Persian Empire defeated the Babylonians in 539 BCE, one year later (538 BCE), King Cyrus of Persia allowed the Jews who were held captive in Babylon to return to their homeland of Judea. Many did return, hoping to re-acclimate themselves to the land and customs of their ancestors. An attempt was made to rebuild the Temple of Jerusalem, which had been utterly decimated by the Babylonians, but this effort was never brought to completion, as the new arrivals from Babylon placed a higher priority on building their own dwelling places. It was Haggai who encouraged the Judeans - twenty years later - to pick up where they left off to give the Lord a proper place of worship, and Zechariah supported his contemporary Haggai's efforts by relating eight visions he received from God as signs that their work would be both worthwhile and rewarded.

THE EIGHT VISIONS

In each vision, an angel explained its message for Zechariah to convey to the Judeans. In the first vision, Zechariah saw four horsemen of different colored steeds stopping in a valley. The angel, who was the first of these riders, asked the Lord how much longer He would be angry with the citizens of Judah. The Lord's response was quite comforting:

> *I have a deep love and concern for Jerusalem, My holy city, and I am very angry with the nations that enjoy quiet and peace. For while I was holding back My anger against My people, those nations made the sufferings of My people worse. So I have come back to Jerusalem to show mercy to the city. My Temple will be restored, and the city will be rebuilt. (Zechariah 1:14-16)*

Zechariah's second vision - the vision of the horns (1:18-21) - showed God's intention to "terrify and overthrow" the nations that had destroyed Judea and scattered its people, and his third vision - the vision of the measuring line (2:1-5) - predicted so much growth for Jerusalem that walls could not contain it; God Himself would protect His city with a wall of fire to encircle it.

In Zechariah's fourth vision - the vision of the High Priest (Zechariah 3:1-10) - the prophet saw Joshua, Jerusalem's High Priest, in filthy attire, standing before an angel of the Lord, about to be accused by Satan. But the angel refused to hear Satan, and exchanged Joshua's dirty clothing with clean clothing. The angel promised that God would send His servant, known as "The Branch," who would

> *...in a single day...take away the sin of this land. (Zechariah 3:9)*

This vision is usually interpreted as God's cleansing of the priesthood, which had grown quite corrupt before the Exile, and His promise to continue the Davidic royal line.

The vision of the lampstand - Zechariah's fifth vision - featured a lampstand (which represented the Temple) and two olive trees (representing Joshua, the High Priest, and Zerubbabel, the governor). The vision indicated that it was the responsibility of these two leaders to complete the reconstruction of God's Temple - and that they would be successful:

> *You will succeed, not by military might or by your own strength, but by My Spirit. Obstacles as great as mountains will disappear before you. You will rebuild the Temple, and as you put the last stone in place, the people will shout, "Beautiful, beautiful!" (Zechariah 4:6-7)*

In his sixth vision, the vision of the flying scroll (Zechariah 5:1-4), Zechariah saw a massive scroll flying through the air. An angel explained to him that the scroll contained curses against thievery and false testimony, and that the curses would find their way into the homes of the guilty throughout the land. The guilty would be removed and their homes left in ruins.

Zechariah's seventh vision (Zechariah 5:5-11) is of a woman sitting in a large basket. The angel who was with him told Zechariah that the basket symbolized the wickedness of the whole nation and the woman was iniquity. The angel pushed the woman down into the basket and closed its lid, after which two other winged angels - who were also women - carried the basket to Babylon, where it would undoubtedly be worshipped.

The final vision experienced by Zechariah consisted of 4 horse-drawn chariots arriving from God's presence. One was red, one black, one white and one dappled. The chariots represented God's justice and they spread to the four corners of the earth to inspect it. Generally, this vision is thought to show Zechariah that the Lord's justice with spread throughout the world - perhaps having begun with the defeat of the Babylonians by the Persians twenty years earlier.

The presence of an angel or angels in each of these visions, coupled with their use of physical symbols and predictions of the future, demonstrate that Zechariah, like Daniel, employed an *apocalyptic* style of writing as he conveyed the messages of God to the people.

ADDITIONAL PREDICTIONS

The last six chapters of the Book of Zechariah contain a number of additional predictions that center around God's punishment of the enemies of His Chosen People and His rescue of Judah, rather than His encouragement of the reconstruction of the Temple. The cities marked for retribution included the Syrian and Philistine towns of Damascus, Tyre, Sidon, Gaza, Ekron, Ashkelon and Hamath. God also expressed His displeasure with the lands of Hadrach (north of Lebanon), Syria, Egypt, Philistia and Assyria.

But God's wrath against the enemies of Judah was overshadowed by His promise to restore Jerusalem and Judah to future glory. One of Zechariah's best know predictions, Christians believe, came true during Jesus' triumphant entry into Jerusalem on Palm Sunday, just five days before His Crucifixion:

Rejoice, Rejoice, people of Zion! Shout for joy, you people of Jerusalem! Look, your king is coming to you! He comes triumphant and victorious, but humble and riding on a donkey - on a colt, the foal of a donkey. (Zechariah 9:9)

Zechariah's words continued to echo God's commitment to forgive, gather and restore the people of Judah as He promised:

The Lord says, "Because of My covenant with you that was sealed by the blood of sacrifices, I will set your people free - free from the waterless pit of exile. Return, you exiles who now have hope; return to your place of safety. Now I tell you that I will repay you twice over with blessing for all you have suffered." (Zechariah 9:11-12)

And this theme continued to resound as Zechariah repeated the words of the Lord:

I will make the people of Judah strong; I will rescue the people of Israel. I will have compassion on them and bring them all back home. They will be as though I had never rejected them. I am the Lord their God; I will answer their prayers. (Zechariah 10:6)

The final chapter of Zechariah offers perhaps the most dramatic oracle of all - describing the time when Yahweh will bring all nations under His reign as He rules from Jerusalem:

The Lord my God will come, bringing all the angels with Him. When that time comes, there will no longer be cold or frost, nor any darkness. There will always be daylight, even at nighttime. When this will happen is known only to the Lord...Then the Lord will be king over all the earth; everyone will worship Him as God and know Him by the same name. (Zechariah 14:6-9)

CHAPTER 21: QUESTIONS FOR REVIEW

1. What details are known of the life of Zechariah?
2. Within the eight visions experienced by Zechariah, what is the symbolic meaning of each of the following: the measuring line, the lampstand, the two olive trees, the flying scroll, the woman and the basket, and the four chariots?
3. What style of writing - similar to that found in the Book of Daniel - is also present in the Book of Zechariah? What are its characteristics?
4. What other cities and lands were mentioned by Zechariah as placed that would also experience the wrath of God?
5. What famous prediction of Zechariah do Christians apply to Jesus?

Chapter Twenty-Two
MALACHI

"I will send you the prophet Elijah"

The final book of Prophetic Literature in the Old Testament is the book of Malachi but, like other books, it is not immune from controversy! In this case, the controversy centers around authorship. The word *malachi* in Hebrew means "my messenger" - raising the question: is this the name of a real person, or is it a designation given to an anonymous author? Others opine that Malachi's words may, in reality, come from the mouth of either Zechariah, Ezra (the High Priest and scribe), Zerubbabel (the governor) or Nehemiah (the architect). The fact is that we may never have closure on this.

The same can be true about the date of Malachi's ministry. The presumption is that Malachi - if he were a real person - was most likely a contemporary of these same four Judeans and that he delivered his prophetic messages in the days after the Temple had been rebuilt and consecrated in 516 BCE. But there are no specific references to historical events that might verify the exact time frame of his writing, either.

Malachi's message might seem rather mundane to today's scriptural audience, but it addressed a growing problem in the post-Exilic world of Judah - the issue of tepid, insincere worship of the Lord. Even in the post-Exilic world of Malachi, animal and grain sacrifices were offered to Yahweh as tokens of devotion. But the people, with the approval of their priests, were cutting corners - and thereby demonstrating not only a degree of personal selfishness but an utter lack of respect for God as well. Perhaps they thought that God would not notice the paucity of their sacrifices - but they were wrong. God addressed this issue through Malachi:

> *A son honors his father, and a servant honors his master. I am your Father - why don't you honor Me? I am your Master - why don't you respect Me? You despise Me, and yet you ask, 'How have we despised You?' This is how - by offering worthless food on My altar. Then you ask, 'How have we failed to respect You?' I will tell you - by showing contempt for My altar.*
>
> *When you bring a blind or sick or lame animal to sacrifice to Me, do you think there's nothing wrong with that? Try giving an animal like that to the*

governor! Would he be pleased with you or grant you any favors? (Malachi 1:6-8)

It was not only the disrespect to God that was rebuked by Malachi, but also the role of the priests in failing to prevent it through proper teaching and example. So God admonished them as well:

It is the duty of priests to teach the true knowledge of God. People should go to them to learn My will, because they are the messengers of the Lord Almighty. But now you priests have turned away from the right path. Your teaching has led many to do wrong. You have broken the covenant I made with you. (Malachi 2:7-8)

Although the Book of Malachi was only four short chapters in length, it covered a lot of ground. Once it finished condemning the insincerity of Judean devotion to God, it also addressed other troubling domestic issues such as divorce, adultery, divination, lying, cheating and insensitivity to the poor:

You have broken your promise to the wife you married when you were young...that you would be faithful to her. Didn't God make you one body and spirit with her?..."I hate divorce", says the Lord God of Israel...The Lord Almighty says, "I will appear among you to judge, and I will testify at once against those who practice magic, against adulterers, against those who give false testimony, those who cheat employees out of their wages, and those who take advantage of widows, orphans and foreigners - against all who do not respect Me." (Malachi 2:14-16, 3:5)

Malachi ends the corpus of Prophetic Literature with a final warning that a day of judgment will be coming to provide final punishment to the wicked and great joy to the righteous, coupled with a reminder that the people of God must always remember and obey the laws and commands given to Moses at Mount Sinai. Malachi's last words from God promise,

> *Before that great and terrible day of the Lord comes, I will send you the prophet Elijah. (Malachi 4:5)*

And today, two and a half millennia later, observant Jews, as they celebrate their freedom from Egyptian slavery at their annual Passover Seder meals, continue to pour a glass of wine and open their front doors as they await the return of Elijah to fulfill this final prophecy. Shalom!

CHAPTER 22: QUESTIONS FOR REVIEW

1. What problems exist in properly identifying Malachi?
2. What was the primary behavior of the Judeans that Malachi hoped to address?
3. What other actions of the Judeans were singled out as wrongful by the Lord?

BIBLIOGRAPHY

Alexander, Pat and David. *Zondervan Handbook to the Bible*. Zondervan Publishing House, 1999, Grand Rapids MI

Hays, J. Daniel. *The Message of the Prophets*. Zondervan, 2010, Grand Rapids MI

Heschel, Abraham J. *The Prophets*. Harper and Row Publishers, 1962, New York NY

Laffey, Alice L. *New Collegeville Bible Commentary: First and Second Kings*, Liturgical Press, 2012, Collegeville MN

Mariottini, Claude. *www.claudemariottini.com*

Miller, Stephen M. *Get Into the Bible: Journey Through the Greatest Story of All Time*. Thomas Nelson Publishers, 1998, Nashville TN

Newland, Mary Reed. *Written on Our Hearts: The Old Testament Story of God's Love*. St. Mary's Press, 1999, Winona MN

Pennock, Michael. *Discovering the Promise of the Old Testament*. Ave Maria Press, 2010, Notre Dame IN

Roberts, William P. *The Prophets Speak Today.* St. Anthony Messenger Press, 1981, Cincinnati OH

Smith, James E. *The Major Prophets.* College Press Publishing Co., 1992, Joplin MO

Walvoord, John F. and Zuck, Roy B. *The Bible Knowledge Commentary: Major Prophets.* David C. Cook Publisher, 2018, Colorado Springs CO

ABOUT THE AUTHOR

Kieran Larkin has been a teacher of theology for the past 40 years. Holding a B.A. in Religious Studies from St. Francis College in Brooklyn and an M.A. in Education from NYU, he has taught courses in Catholic high school ranging from morality, social justice and comparative religions to Christology and Biblical themes. He has also been an active liturgical participant throughout his adult life as both a lector and eucharistic minister. He has a special passion for the lives and ministries of the prophets, who he considers to be particularly heroic and inspirational.

www.ingramcontent.com/pod-product-compliance
Lightning Source LLC
Chambersburg PA
CBHW071305110526
44591CB00010B/781